HEAL MY BROKEN HEART O GOD

FINDING LIFE AFTER THE LOSS OF A LOVED ONE

WILLIAM T MOORE

HEAL MY BROKEN HEART O GOD: FINDING LIFE
AFTER THE LOSS OF A LOVED ONE

By William T Moore

ISBN: 978-1-7373750-2-9

Published in Clearwater, FL

Table of Contents

THE LOSS OF A SPOUSE OR CHILD, OR A DIVORCE

I hope this book brings healing to the broken hearted and those crushed in spirit. This will encompass the loss of a spouse, the loss of a child, or the tearing apart of those who were joined in marriage, to became one again. The healing process is the same for all three. Some of the things written in this book will not apply to everyone's situation. All the topics on receiving healing are applicable to everyone. My hope and prayer is that everyone who has been through one of these situations receives healing to the fullest.

Pray this prayer out loud:

Father God, I come before you in the name of Jesus. Help me to see in this book the things that you have for me to do. Give me courage and boldness like I've never had before. Break off all the fog that surrounds my situation now. Give me the eyes to see, and ears to hear, what you have for me in this book. Help me, Lord Jesus, to be healed. Help me to find you and help me to live a life blessed with abundance. Come, Holy Spirit.

Pray all the prayers in this book pray out loud. Praying out loud puts it into the atmosphere. It says I am serious about this I want Father God to move on my behalf.

CHAPTER 1
WHY, GOD?

Why? What went wrong? Where was God Almighty? Why is this happening to me? Did Father God know this would be happening to me, to us, now? If you're like me, you have asked all these questions, and maybe some I haven't asked yet.

Losing your loved one was probably the worst day of your life. Years ago, I remember our five-year-old grandson throwing himself into a chair and exclaiming, "This is the worst day of my life! My life is ruined." It wasn't, he's had worse, and his life hasn't been ruined.

For me, losing Kate was the worst day of my life. I can't think of any day that has been worse than the day I left the hospital. I knew my life wasn't ruined, but it sure was tossed on its ear. Now what? Can I continue? Do I want to move forward? Can I continue living without one of the best things that's happened in my life to date?

What do I know?

1. God is my Father God
2. God is love. God LOVES me.
3. God is good.
4. Father God is the creator of heaven and earth.
5. Jesus loves me, this I know.
6. Holy Spirit has a plan to prosper me and not harm me.
7. The Father does not lie.
8. Father God, Jesus, and Holy Spirit are faithful.

9. The Bible is the inerrant word of God. No errors are found in it. No lies are found in it.

What about the things I don't know? I don't know why God does some things and not others. The things I don't understand are called "Mysteries of God." If I know for sure 1, 2 and 3, then all the things I don't know will be taken care of. If there is no mystery. God is predictable. If God is predictable. Then I will fall into the trap of using. formula is to get him to do things for me.

Here we are now. Parts of this book have been written trying to navigate through the first year of life without Kate. That very first week, I had to make the decision to continue living life to the fullest. And then the question arose, "How do I do that?" It's been some time now, the only thing I can say is I need to get up out of bed every day and make your bed. Why? Because making the bed might be the only thing I accomplish that day. It has gotten a lot better. Goals have been set, and I have learned to function on my own. I wonder about that last one.

You will make it. You will come out on the other side of this experience whole and healthy if you decide right now, "I will make it." In the early days, you will be wondering how you are going to make it. If you're like me, I was asking, "Why was I ever born?" The rough patches during those first couple weeks were the worst. I knew I had to power through, trying to grasp anything that was positive. Life will get better. You will have to work at it. There will be good days and bad days. There will be well meaning people saying stupid stuff. Grace, grace, *grace*. They have no idea what you're going through. They have no idea how to help you. You will have to take charge of your own recovery. There will be times when you just want to assume the fetal position and give up. That's when you need to pray:

O God, O God, O God, have mercy on me because I can't do this by myself. Help, Lord; come, Holy Spirit; fill me. Fill me up again. Show me your mercy and grace. Show me what to do next. I don't have a clue. In Jesus' name, help.

Mercy is the love of God not giving you what you deserve. Grace is the kindness of God giving you what you didn't deserve.

I have been praying my way through life since I found Jesus, or Jesus found me. It's best if you say these prayer sections out loud. Don't be shy. If you need to shout them at the top of your lungs, Father God won't be shocked, and Holy Spirit is not a fragile little dove that can be frightened away.

THE QUESTION: WHERE WAS GOD WHILE ALL THIS WAS HAPPENING?

You know the answer. The Sunday school answer. The answer every preacher and all your friends are going to tell you: "God was right there through the whole thing." And if you're like me, you smile and nod your head in agreement, thinking, "Bull crap."

Acts 17:26 is my attempt to explain exactly where God was when life was falling apart:

> *"From one man he made all the nations, that they should inhabit the whole earth; and * he marked out their appointed times in history and the boundaries of their lands. (NIV)*

having determined allotted periods and the boundaries of their dwelling places."

"From one man, Adam, he made every man and women and every race of humanity, and he spread us over all the earth. *He set the boundaries of people and nations, determining their appointed times in history." (TPT)

God was before the beginning of time. God was before the creation of earth. God Almighty was before everything. There has never been a time when God did not exist. Before the earth was formed and the stars were hung in the sky, Father God, creator of heaven and earth, knew you. He knew the exact time you would come into existence. He knew the exact place where you would live; not just the city, but the street and house number where you would live. And he knows where you will be two years from now.

God was before time. Somewhere in there, he decided to have creation, the Genesis Story. And on this timeline, he knew the exact minute you would be born, and he knows the exact time when your life will end. Everything and everyone that has come into being since creation, Father God knew it was going to happen.

Father God was before the line started, and he will be after the line ends.

We don't become angels. We become spirit beings who are in heaven to rule and reign with Jesus. Now in my peewee thinking, my finite thinking, there must be a way for us to know when we're all going to get together for church in heaven. I had to stop writing this for a minute or two to get myself back together because I cracked up laughing. Every now and then, I have a thought about God that's completely wrong, and I just crack up. And I have a feeling, although I don't know this for sure, that Holy Spirit just got a good laugh.

Did Father God know that your spouse or child was going to leave you at this point in time? The answer is of course he did. It was part of the plan that he had for you and for them. But why? Could he not have kept this whole thing from happening? The answer is yes. But for some reason, here we are. I wish there was some way I could convey the agony I'm in as I put this on paper. Part of me is screaming at God. Another piece of me is torn up. And then part of me is trusting God to see me through this and into what comes next. Was God in the hospital room when Kate went home to be with him? Absolutely. Did he blink for a minute and lose sight of what was happening? Absolutely not. He knows the exact situation that is happening. He knows the exact situation as it is now. He knows the exact outcome of your future. And he knows the outcome of your life and all that is coming your way. Both the good times and bad times. Help, Lord.

Pray this out loud: *Father God, I come before you in the name of Jesus. You were before time. You are in time right now, and when time is over, you are also there. Help me to grasp this idea. I know that you were with me. I know that you are with me now. I know that you will see me through this next week and the next six months. Help me to find you in all of this. Show me how to get healed from all this pain. You are my heavenly Father, who has greater concern and greater love for me than my earthly father could ever experience. Come, Lord Jesus, and heal me. Help me to fall in love with you more and more every day. I don't know how much more of this I can take. Come, Holy Spirit. Help.*

Chapter 2
OUR STORY

The following was written on the day Kate moved on to be with Jesus. Kate had been in the hospital having a brain tumor removed. She never woke up after the operation.

I was trying to begin the healing process. On the way home, I started to talk with God:

Kate just died. Or should I say her vital signs stopped being evident or her body gave up trying to live without a spirit. I'm on my way home from the hospital. It's raining, I mean really raining. Can't see the car in front of me raining. I'm trying to kick the can of mourning down street. So I'm trying to get angry at somebody, anybody, but it's not working. I'm thinking the doctors—I should be mad at them. But I know that they had done everything they possibly could have. The nursing staff and doctors in NICU were the best. The doctor who did the operation is one of the best in the state from what I am told by nurse friends. I figure the only one left to be mad at is God. I started complaining to God, our loving, kind, and compassionate God, and He said, "Did I not heal her? She is here with me right now, whole, and healthy. She never saw death; she never felt it sting." I moaned back, "But she's not here with me. I'm never going to pray again." Then Holy Spirit said, "I will miss our mornings together, not to mention our talks throughout the day." I am still trying get mad at God. I made it home. I'm sitting in the driveway, and it is still pouring down rain, and the cloud cover is thick. I muttered to myself, "Thirty seconds—just stop the rain for thirty seconds." BAM. The rain stopped instantly.

The sun came out. I jumped out of the car, got to the porch, and the rain started to come down in buckets again. I never really have gotten mad or angry at anyone.

We had a celebration of life for Kate, and the church was packed. Kate had been involved in many things. She was part of a stitching group at Crafty Framer. She stopped going because her hands started to have a little shake and her eyes couldn't see. She missed those ladies. About five years earlier, we wanted something to do together, so we took a watercolor painting course at the Pinellas Park Art Society. Later she became a board member. She became interested in alcohol ink and started teaching a class.

Many people from all different backgrounds came to her celebration of life: work friends, art friends, stitching friends, homegroups going back thirty years. Some of the people commented that they had never been to a Christian celebration of life. The religious friends weren't sure if the balloons were a good idea. Everyone present heard that Father God loves them from three different speakers in three different ways.

There is no right way to get healed from the loss of a loved one there is only your way. I have also found that the stages of grieving may not be the same for each of us. Elizabeth Kubler Ross has a theory that the five stages of grieving that a terminally ill patient goes through. The five stages are: denial, anger, bargaining, depression, and acceptance. In the past they have been equated with someone going through the grieving process. There is an assortment of emotions you can go through, and they are in no particular order and can be repeated. Therefore, you and Father God need to work through this together. God in His infinite wisdom knows exactly what you need to come out whole and healthy on the other side of this. It's your personalized healing. It has been designed specifically for you. There will be helpful people along the way, and there will be people who only think they're helping. Quietly sort through the process you are in. There will be times when you will get hung up. Pray and praise God for what is next. Always try to keep moving forward. Keep in mind the people around you are well-intentioned, but unless they've been there, they have no idea how to help. Even if they have been through this, their experience is theirs, and your experience is yours. Everyone has a different way of going through loss. Every now and then, one of them might come up with something helpful.

Chapter 3
DOES GOD LOVE ME?

It sure doesn't feel like it.

Pray this out loud.

Father God, make the hurt go away. There is a hole in my life. Help me to get healed. I know you love me. (I think.) Help me to see, feel, and know your love for me, in Jesus' name.

1 John 4:16b says, "God is love."

Think about it. The Creator of heaven and earth, Awesome Lord God Almighty, is love. How great is that? Someone once said our view of God is heavily influenced by our interaction with our earthly father. Father God is not like your earthly father, who may or may not have been a loving, caring and compassionate father. In my childhood, I experienced unconditional love most of the time. And other times, it was love with conditions. If you do _____, then you will get love. That was never stated that way, but we all know how to do it. In the next couple of verses, we will see how great the love of Father God is. And it is focused on you. Here is a God who is running the universe, hearing all the prayers that are being prayed right now, and he cares about little old you. How great is that?

1 John 3:1a says, "See what great love the Father has lavished on us, that we should be called children of God!"

From the word "lavished," means generous and extravagant it is from an old French word *Lavache* meaning deluge or torrent, referring to rain. The word lavished gives us the picture of someone standing under a waterfall and hundreds of gallons of love pouring over them. At the end of the football game, the winning coach is lavished with Gatorade. That picture doesn't even come close to depicting the outpouring of love God has for us. His love is greater than any love you could pour out on any other person. We really have no concept of how great the love of the Father is for us. Many of us have no idea how to experience this unconditional love. Holy Spirit can wash over you with this great love.

Pray: *Come Holy Spirit. Wash over me with the love of the Father, in Jesus' name, please.* (Take 10 minutes, close your eyes, and picture yourself under the waterfall of love.)

> *"Dear friends, let us love one another, for love is from God. And everyone who loves has been born of God and knows God. 8 The one who does not love does not know God, for God is love." 1 John 4:7-8*

Here is one of the great challenges in the Bible. We are to love one another, even those around us who are prickly. That is hard to do. Everyone who loves has been born of God and knows God. We love because he loved us. We have been born of God. Another way to think of it is we have been born *into* God. And once again, we see that God is love.

Pray this: *O God, help me to love like you love me. Help me to love without conditions, in Jesus' name.*

> *"There is no fear in love. But perfect love drives out fear, because fear has to do punishment." 1 John 4:1 (NIV)*

You should never be afraid in coming to Father God. God is love; He understands. He doesn't have a knee jerk reaction when you mess up. Remember that time when you really screwed something up? I can still see my mother's bony finger pointing at me while she explained what I just did that was so horrendous. The God of the Old Testament and the God of the New Testament are the same. Our God has given us Jesus as the way to come to him. When God looks at us, he sees Jesus in us. You can commit the most heinous sin possible, and God looks at you through Jesus. He doesn't even see your sin or remember it. In the Kingdom of God, the sin never happened. He sees Jesus paying the price for your sin. When we confess our sins, it is like our sin never occurred. Father God loves you so much that every sin you have ever committed, and every sin you will ever commit, the price has been paid by Jesus. God loves you more than you can imagine. And he knows how you were made and the condition of the world we live in. He knows our sin nature, that part of us that slips into sin so easily, sometimes willfully and in full knowledge that we are about to sin. And he still loves us. We are in awe of who God is and what he has done for us. God is Love; therefore, there is no fear in God.

> *"Love is patient, love is kind. It does not envy, it does not boast, it is not proud. It does not dishonor others, it is not self-seeking, it is not*

easily angered, it keeps no record of wrongs.
Love does not delight in evil but rejoices with the
truth. It always protects, always trusts, always
hopes, always perseveres. Love never fails."
1 Corinthians 13:4-8a (NIV)

Try this on. God is patient. God is kind. God does not envy. God is not self-seeking. God is not easily angered. God keeps no record of wrongs. God rejoices in the truth. God always protects, always trusts, always hopes, always perseveres. God never fails. This First Corinthians passage gives us a picture of who God is and what he is all about. This picture of God, our loving, kind Father, is much different than what the world thinks of God.

God is patient. He does not get upset when we mess up.

God is kind. He never does anything in anger or for any other wrong reasons.

God is not easily angered. It takes a whole lot to get him angry.

God keeps no record of wrongs. He's not up there with a ledger keeping track of the things we do wrong. The minute we ask for forgiveness, we are forgiven, and he doesn't know it happened. He doesn't forget it. In heaven, it never happened. Unlike us who never forget. We forgive, but the residue of it remains deep down in the recess of our being unless we forgive unconditionally.

"As far as the east is from the west, so far does he remove our transgressions from us."
Psalm 103:12

God always protects. He loves us so much, and he will put a hedge of protection around us to keep us safe. Does Father God really love *you*? I can't think of many things worse than not knowing if God loves me just the way I am right now. The day you prayed the prayer of salvation, you walked into the fulness of the Lord God Almighty's love for you. His love is unconditional and has no boundaries. The Father doesn't love us because we get it right. He loves you no less or no more than he does right now. You can't get "more better" or "more saved" to make him love you more.

Does Father God really love me? The answer is Father God loves you more than you can imagine. I have no idea why, because I don't measure up to any standard of holiness to be in his presence. It's all because of what Jesus did for me that I have right standing with God. Thank you, Jesus. God, in his wisdom, made a way for us to come before him.

"For God so loved the world that he gave his one and only Son, that whoever believes in him shall not perish but have eternal life." John 3:16 (NIV)

"For God so loved YOU so much that he gave his One and Only Son, JESUS, that if YOU believe in him YOU will not perish but have eternal life." (John 3:16, my paraphrase)

God gave this broad statement that if you believe Jesus is his son, Father God will give you eternal life. For me, all it took was hearing the words that God loved me.

Holy Spirit came and impacted my heart. I was changed by a fifteen-minute story of how much God loved the boy David and was with him when he slew his giant, Goliath. There is no end to the love and compassion Father God has for you.

I have a friend who attended our home Bible study group. After the third or fourth visit, he made an incredible statement. "Aren't you afraid that the way you people talk to God will make him mad?" It took a minute, then I saw what was happening. His view of God was off a little. I asked the question, "How do you see God?" "God is waiting for me to screw something up, so he can release bad things on me. God is waiting with a club, watching for me to sin." It was a fifteen-minute conversation, but these two statements summarize it.

Pray this prayer: *Father of all creation, give me an accurate view of who you are and who I am in you. Break off all the lies I have mistakenly believed. Come, Holy Spirit. In Jesus' name, do this. Open my eyes for me to see myself the way you do. Please, do it now, in Jesus' name.*

Take a few minutes, wait, and listen.

Psalms 103:1-5, 8-13, 17a

Praise the Lord, my soul;
all my inmost being, praise His holy name.
2 Praise the Lord, my soul,
and forget not all His benefits—
Who forgives all your sins
and heals all your diseases,

3 Who redeems your life from the pit
and crowns you with love and compassion,
4 Who satisfies your desires with good things
so that your youth is renewed like the eagle's.
8 The Lord is compassionate and gracious,
slow to anger, abounding in love.
9 He will not always accuse,
nor will he harbor His anger forever;
10 he does not treat us as our sins deserve
or repay us according to our iniquities.
(sin committed by our ancestors going back four
generations)
11 For as high as the heavens are above the earth,
so great is His love for those who fear him;
12 as far as the east is from the west,
so far has he removed our transgressions from us.
13 As a father has compassion on His children,
so the Lord has compassion on those who fear him;
17 But from everlasting to everlasting
the Lord's love is with those who fear him.

Keep in mind all of Psalms 103 was written before Jesus. How much better it is for us who have Jesus? *Hallelujah*!

Here is the difference between sin, transgression, and iniquities:

Sin is the wrong we do, not knowing that what we did was sin.

Transgression is knowing that a particular activity is sin and doing it regardless.

Iniquities are the sins committed by your ancestors: your parents, your grandparents, and your great

18

grandparents. It is hard for 21st century Christians to get their head wrapped around that the sins of their ancestors to the third and fourth generation are still laid on them. The screwups that your great grandfather did are still coming back to haunt you even if you never even knew him. "But wait, Bill, that's not fair," you might think. However, Father God forgives our iniquities, the sins of our ancestors, if we ask.

> 10 he does not treat us as our sins deserve
> or repay us according to our iniquities.
> 11 For as high as the heavens are above the earth,
> so great is his love for those who fear him;
> 12 as far as the east is from the west,
> so far has he removed our transgressions from us. Psalms 103: 10-12 (NIV)

The word "fear" is sprinkled through this Psalm. In the year 1611, the King James translators used the word fear throughout the Old Testament. The word doesn't translate well. It is much bigger. It means respect, reverence, fear, and awe, all rolled into one word. We don't have one word to adequately translate the word for "fear."

Have you prayed the prayer of salvation? The answer probably is yes. Here is prayer compiled from many sources, starting with the early church fathers. They were serious about getting a person saved, cleansed, and filled all in the same day, all at the same time.

Chapter 4
Prayer of Salvation

Father God, I come before you in the name of Jesus, the name that's above all names. Thank you, Father God, for letting me experience the love of Jesus resting on me. Thank you, Father, for forgiving all my sins. Right now, I renounce all my sins, and the sins of my ancestors. Because you have forgiven me, right now, I forgive everyone who has ever sinned against me, done me wrong, or harmed me in any way (name them).

I believe that I am forgiven. I believe that Jesus died on the cross for my sins, and on the third day, he arose from the dead.

Come, Holy Spirit, fill me. Reside in me. Help me to experience and share the love of Jesus with others.

Right now, I renounce all contact and break all ties with Satan, the occult, or any secret society. I declare that Satan has no more hold over my life or my family's lives. I break every curse over my life, my ancestor's lives, and my living family's lives in Jesus' name. I receive all the blessings available to me and my family through Christ Jesus.

Jesus is Lord.

Jesus is risen from the dead.

I am forgiven.

I have been set free from the law of sin and death.

God is my Father, and all his blessing are mine.

This prayer is longer than most prayers people have prayed for their Salvation. It is a compilation of many different prayers prayed over centuries.

The bold sentences are meant to be shouted as a declaration of what just happened, as if you are letting the whole world know your life is different from this point on. Go back and say this prayer out loud with passion, and when you get to the bold sentences, shout them, and let all those around you know what has just happened to you.

CHAPTER 5
EXPERIENCING THE
LOVE OF THE FATHER

In the second sentence, the prayer of salvation mentions experiencing the love of Father God. I assumed, just like me, that everyone experienced the love of the Father when they accepted Jesus. In my maturity, I have found that some people have questioned if they have experienced the Father's love. Let's take a minute and practice being in the presence of the love of Father God.

Find yourself a comfortable place, quiet, free from the distractions of the outside world. Dial down. What does that mean? Dialing down is releasing all your anxieties, fears, stress, and anything else that can come between you and Father God right now in this moment. Quiet your mind. Don't empty your mind, like they do in Eastern religion. Take captive every thought. You might need to say the words, "I take captive every thought in the name of Jesus. Thoughts, be quiet, be still, hush." Say this out loud.

Now pray this:
Come, Holy Spirit. Let me experience the love of the Father. Let the love of Father God wash over me. Heal me. Fill me with your love in Jesus' name.

Take some time, 15 to 20 minutes, to let Father's love wash over you. If you feel you're not experiencing anything, try again later. Quieting your mind takes practice. Many of us have never experienced a quiet mind. We always have many thoughts running through it all the time. I have one friend who said that he has five trains running down five different tracks, running through his mind all at the same time, all the time. His last name is Train.

Chapter 6
THE PAIN

I have never experienced pain like this in my whole life. My four grandparents are gone and so are my mother and father. The pain I experienced at the loss of Kate was all consuming, and for the most part, overwhelming most of the time. I have experienced physical pain, major hurts, and wounds. But compared to losing my best friend and lover, those wounds were a piece of cake. The overwhelming dark shadow that followed me around was relentless until I got a grip on how to get healed. The pain comes and goes. At first, it's all consuming. Then I would have times when I would think I was getting ahead of it. Then, out of nowhere, it would come back with a vengeance, and into the deep, dark hole of grief I would fall. The phrase "time heals all wounds" is false. As time goes by, you can get yourself into a better place, but the reality is you need healing, supernatural, miraculous healing from Holy Spirit. This healing is not hard to get, but you need to be relentless at keeping it. I have prayed this prayer:

Lord Jesus, come heal my wounded flesh, and heal my wounded spirit. Heal that place where _____ used to reside, which is now missing. Heal me, Father God, in Jesus' name.

In the beginning, I was praying this almost hourly:
Come, Holy Spirit. Heal this hurt. Take the pain away. Heal me now, Help, Lord Jesus.

Chapter 7
THE WOUND
WHY DOES IT HURT SO BAD?

Here's the problem as I see it:

> "*For this reason a man shall leave his father and mother 8 (and be united to his wife. (NIV), and the two will become one flesh.*" *(Mark 10:7-8a)* NASB95

The loss of anyone you love leaves a hole in your flesh where part of you is missing and needs to be healed.

Your life is circling the toilet bowl, and you are riding a turd raft, and there is nothing you can do about it. (I have made seven revisions of this sentence and this is the least graphic of them all.) You find yourself being half of what you used to be. The question is, "How do I become whole again?" For years, you and your spouse (or you and your child) had been living and thriving together. Suddenly, you find yourself alone. Suddenly you find yourself with a big piece missing.

My prayer was this:

"Lord Jesus, get me through this hour. I need help getting through this next week. Get me through this next six months. Come, Holy Spirit. Heal my wounded flesh and heal my crushed spirit in Jesus' name."

Of course, this was a daily prayer, and even sometimes an hourly prayer, just to get me through to the day. Just to get me through the next hour and through the melt downs. Waves of remorse and grief would flow over me at the oddest times. I could be driving down the road, or watching TV, and a smell, a sound, or seeing something would trigger feelings, and into the depths I would fall. I asked a friend, "Does this ever stop?" He responded, "It's been seven years, and I've been remarried for five years, and just last week I had a thought about my late wife, and into the black hole of grief I fell. Those times are getting fewer and fewer. I don't know if it ever goes away. It does get better. You can find yourself again."

I prayed this: *"Lord Jesus, make me whole again. Come, Holy Spirit. Heal my wounded soul. Heal my wounded spirit. Heal that part of me that is missing. Fill me with your Holy Spirit."*

I have prayed that many times, and sometimes in the same hour. I think you never really get over losing a loved one. Life as you know it has changed, and it will never be the same. You will never be the same. But you can get better. Life gets better. What you're going through and what you're feeling is normal. You will make it.

Some people will be saying to themselves, or their friends will say, "Steady on, have a stiff upper lip," or you think, "I can bull my way through this, move on, get over it. With dogged determination, I will not be sucked into this pit of grief and despair. I don't need to grieve." Don't go there. Emotions can be something few guys want to deal with especially his own—*no, not ever.* Keep in mind that the emotional center in a man's brain is about as big as a thumb nail. A woman's emotional center is about the size of a walnut and every thought runs through that center. (Wondrium Oct 12,2018, "How do the Brains of Men and Women Differ?) A man's thoughts can run through the emotional center, but they can use the bypass when necessary and it's always necessary. Men, do not stuff your emotions. You have been wounded, torn in two. Deal with it. I remember a drill instructor yelling in my ear, "Get your head out of your ass!"

Men and women, take time to remember all the good times you had together. Mourn the times you won't have together. There are two ways to do this. The first is to make this a painful process. The second is to make it a celebration of the times you had together. Remember and rejoice. The first time you do this, it will be very painful. The next time, make it a celebration. The result you want in six months or a year from now is that when you remember that time, it puts a smile on your face. The first couple times of remembering the good times will be difficult. But you have to get past that so that when one of the kids brings something up, you're not thrown into a pit of remorse and loss.

There are several things that can happen when you don't deal with the emotions of losing someone. The obvious one is that you don't become whole again. You remain half a person. You get stuck. Consequently, you become comfortable with a life of mourning, sadness, and grief. This becomes your new normal. You wake up in the morning, and you can't find a reason to get out of bed. This is okay for a little while, but you need to find your new place in life. Remember, it starts with baby steps. Reestablish yourself; redefine yourself.

Another big trap of the enemy is thinking, "If I could find somebody to fill this hole in my life, I'll be okay." Make a dogged determination to get through the first year without looking for love again. Never get married without spending a year dating. I've seen it happen several times, that Knight in Shining Armor or that Princess in Glimmering White can fool you for six months. If you can stick it out for a year, you will find out what they're really like. Are they faking it? Are they too good to be true? "He goes to church with me," you might think, but after a whirlwind romance, you find that he no longer goes to church at all. It takes time to find out what makes a person tick. Don't let the enemy trick you into thinking you know everything about them in three or four months. It's a whole new world out there. Find out as much as you can about them, even pay a little money do a background check.

One young lady in our singles group thought she found Mr. Right. After five months, they were engaged to be married. A week before the big day, it was discovered that he was being sought by authorities for sexual assault. She had two children.

Find things that you can do with family and friends while you are single. Join a group. Learn something new. Never give up. One of the most tragic things that can happen to an individual or a family is losing a loved one. You must fight to get healed. Find yourself again in this new life as a single person.

John 10:10b says, "Jesus came that you might have life and have it abundantly."

The whole verse is this:

> "Jesus said, *'The thief came to steal, kill and destroy. I came that you might have life and have it abundantly.'"* (NASB95)

Don't let Satan destroy you through this life event that half of us are going to go through. You can come out the other side whole and healthy. It will take work. It will take planning. It will take praying. And it will take fighting to find your place in this new paradigm (world view).

I encourage you during those first few weeks to find two people, of your gender, who will pray for you consistently for a year. Prayer is an emotional experience and can create emotional ties between people. Because of the emotional ties that prayer can create, it's best that your pray-ers are of the same gender as you. These two people will need to pray for you weekly in person for the first two or three months. The prayer is for healing. They should pray just like they would pray for any person who was hurt, just like you would pray for someone with a heart condition. Pray for healing. Try this prayer model.

1. "Where does it hurt?" You already know part of the answer—half of you is missing. You need to be whole again, but there will be new stuff.

2. They should ask Holy Spirit how they should pray for you. "Holy Spirit, what do you want to heal today?" Take a minute or two and listen to what Holy Spirit has to say.

3. Out loud, ask Holy Spirit to show you how and what to pray.

4. After praying, ask the question, "Is anything happening? Do you feel anything: heat, tingling, or vibration, or something like

electricity?" You are looking for evidence that Holy Spirit is doing something. I have seen people with sweat running down their face, shaking and coughing, and when asked the question, "Is anything happening?" they say, "No." It's great when you can see something, or they feel something, but it doesn't happen all the time. Other signs something is going on include that their eyes closed, and their eye lids are twitching; beads of perspiration; sneezing/coughing; or a slight trembling.

5. Ask Holy Spirit for a scripture verse to meditate on until next week.

6. *Praise.* Praise Jesus for what he did, and for what he is about to do. The three of you should praise God throughout the week for the healing you are getting.

Some people don't know how to receive a healing or how to receive prayer. First, begin by expecting to be healed. Get comfortable; sit or stand. Relax, dial down, take a few deep breaths; with each deep breath, let all anxiousness flow out of you. Clear your mind of self-talk. Tell yourself, "Mind, be at peace; be still." Say it out loud. The one receiving prayer should be still, not praying in the Spirit, not reciting scripture verses. Relax and receive. Give Holy Spirit a chance.

Chapter 8
FOR YOUR FRIENDS

THIS IS THE PAIN YOUR FRIEND IS EXPERIENCING

This next section is for your friends; copy it and hand it to them.

Dear Friend,

Unless you've been here, you have no idea what is happening to your friend. If you have been here, but have worked through it the wrong way, you may not be as helpful as you think you are. Healing from the loss of a spouse or child is personal. There is no one way to go through the process. There is only the plan Jesus has specifically for your friend. Here is what has happened. Your friend has been wounded by the worst kind of hurt—the loss of a family member. In the 21st century industrial world, we hide our grief. We are so shallow that we don't want to be around others who are hurting. We want to avoid grief, pain, and hurting people. Here is what is happening. With the loss of a family member, the heart is broken, the spirit is crushed, and the person who was whole is now torn in half. What needs to be healed? The broken heart, the crushed spirit, and the half-person need to be made whole.

We don't know how to grieve. We want our friend to get over it: "cheer up; get over it. Stiff upper lip," or "I don't want to talk about your loss because it makes me sad, and it could happen to me." We will do almost anything not to be sad, especially if it's someone else's sadness we're around. Some people don't deal with pain or hardship at all. It is like we have made an inner vow to be happy and cheerful even during the most painful times of our lives. We can't let anyone see us hurting. "I can't deal with your grief," we feel, "Therefore, see you in a couple months." Then there are those who want you to never heal. They want you to suffer with them forever: "Let me tell you how badly I am hurting, so that you can feel sorry for me also."

> *"Blessed are those who mourn, for they will be comforted." Matthew 5:4 (NIV)*

If you don't mourn, you don't get comforted. Mourning is part of the life that we have been born into. We don't know how to mourn anymore. Mourning is recognizing part of you is missing. They were a part of your life, and now they are not. I don't want this, but here I am.

Be aware that your friend may be hurting because they feel abandoned. This is one of many emotions someone living in the fog of grief may feel. If they don't have a grasp of the love Father God has for them, it may be as simple as asking Holy Spirit to come show them the Father's love.

Your friend has been told to find two people, of the same gender as themself, who will commit to a year of prayer for them. Prayer is an emotional experience and can create emotional ties between people. Because of the emotional ties that prayer can create, it's best that the pray-ers are the same gender as they are. The two of you will need to pray for your friend weekly in person for the first two or three months. The prayer is for healing. You should pray just like you would pray for any person who was hurt—just like you would pray for someone with a heart condition. Pray for healing. Try this prayer model.

1. "Where does it hurt?" You already know part of the answer—half of you is missing. You need to be whole again, but there will be new stuff.

2. They should ask Holy Spirit how they should pray for you. "Holy Spirit, what do you want to heal today?" Take a minute or two and listen to what Holy Spirit has to say.

3. Out loud, ask Holy Spirit to show you how and what to pray. "Holy Spirit come show us how to pray. Help us to see what you see."

4. After praying, ask the question, "Is anything happening? Do you feel anything: heat, tingling, or vibration, or something like electricity?" You are looking for evidence that Holy Spirit is doing something. I have seen people with sweat running down their face, shaking and coughing, and when asked the question, "Is anything happening?" they say, "No." It's great when you can see something, or they feel something, but it doesn't happen all the time. Other signs something is going on include that their eyes closed, and their eye lids are twitching; beads of perspiration; sneezing/coughing; or a slight trembling.

5. Ask Holy Spirit for a scripture verse to meditate on until next week.

6. *Praise.* Praise Jesus for what he did, and for what he is about to do. The three of you should praise

God throughout the week for the healing you are getting.

In those first ten days, the only question you should ask your friend is, "What can I do for you?" The response might be, "Could you take the trash out?" During this time, your friend has no idea what they need or what needs to be done. They are on autopilot, coasting through life on a roller coaster. For example, most of us are unprepared for funeral arrangements. Someone may need to help them walk through the funeral process.

The best thing you can do is come alongside with words of encouragement, and every now and then, we need to go do _____. This is to get away from the house. Go out to lunch. Go to a movie. Get ice cream. Walk in the park. Drag races, shooting, tea party, shopping, snorkeling, helping someone else, et cetera, are all options.

> *"Rejoice with those who rejoice; mourn with those who mourn." Romans 12:15 (NIV)*
>
> *"Weeping in the night, this is a season" Psalms 30:5 (NIV)*
>
> *"Those who sow in tears will reap with songs of joy." Psalms 126:4 (NIV).*

The enemy wants your friend to make grieving a lifestyle. Don't let them get stuck in their pain. Some of us will lie down in the Valley of the Shadow of Death rather than keep walking. At this point, they may need a lot of encouragement. The more stubborn of us may need to get a kick in the butt, figuratively.

Chapter 9
STAGES OF GRIEVING

STAGES OF GRIEVING AS I SEE THEM

1. HOPELESSNESS. Oh, the pain. Shock. Confusion and disorientation. It's hopeless. You don't understand what just happened. The wound is open, and you feel every twinge. It feels like blood is flowing from an artery. O God, where are you? O God, where were you? There is no getting over this—you must go through it. It feels like you're in the Valley of the Shadow of Death. The prayer is *"Help, Lord Jesus. I don't understand."*

2. GRIEVING. You are getting accustomed to the pain. Reality is setting in. You are still floundering around, wondering if you will make it. It feels like the bleeding has stopped, but the wound could open up at any time. Stiches are in but they may not hold if you move around. Why, God? The prayer is, *"Help, Lord, I need to see you in all this mess."*

#*%#$@ This doesn't get a number or a name. It appears and disappears. It's mourning. You float in and out of despair, loneliness, and loss. You are in a fog, a haze, and you feel numb. Hopelessness is banging on the door. Jesus, are you out there? *The prayer is, "Lord Jesus, I saw the light at the end of the tunnel, but now I don't anymore. Help, Lord Jesus."*

Be careful not to get stuck here. Recognize your condition and ask for help: *"Help, Lord Jesus. I can't seem to get out of my own way. This fogginess is consuming me. I need your help to move on. Fogginess in the name of Jesus go. Blahs in the name of Jesus go."*

4. KNOWING. You are in the state of knowing. Mourning continues, but you *know* your life has changed. Clarity has come, and you just might make it. It feels like a scab has formed, and healing has begun. The prayer is, *"Lord Jesus, I want to be healed. Come, heal my spirit and soul. Make me whole again. Broken heart, be healed. Crushed spirit, come alive again in Jesus' name."*

5. HEALING. Healing has begun. You are seriously and diligently seeking Jesus to heal your broken heart, heal your wounded spirit, and make your body whole again. The glimpses of hope are more and more prevalent. I can make it. I will make it. The prayer is, *"Come, Holy Spirit. I must be healed. Come and lead me in the way this is going to happen in Jesus' name. I am blessed."*

Write this on paper

I CAN MAKE IT. I WILL MAKE IT THROUGH WITH JESUS

Tape it to the bathroom mirror, the steering wheel, the TV, or the refrigerator.

Chapter 10
WHAT TO DO

I took two pastoral counseling courses at Southeastern University in Lakeland, Florida, and came to the realization, over the years, that I was terrible at counseling. Then God showed me to come alongside the person, hang out, and pray with them. Be a cheerleader: "You can do it. Fight, fight." I shared verses that Holy Spirit brought to mind, not in an authoritarian way, but as a friend who will not give up. Become an exhorter: Listen, cry, laugh, pray, share life. It's going to get better. You will make it.

In John 11 we get a look at Lazarus rising from the dead. Jesus was deeply grieved. And Jesus knew that in a short while, he was going to raise Lazarus from the dead. Despite this, Jesus connected with grief. Jesus connects with each of us where we are. Read John 11 with the eyes of Jesus. His close friend has died. Lazarus's sisters are mourning. The village was mourning. What did Jesus do? Verse35 says "Jesus wept." He came alongside the others. Jesus entered their grieving.

Grieving is for a season. You can't allow yourself to enter a lifestyle of grief. The time of deep grieving should last seven to ten days. The next thirty days are grieving but not as deeply. Get out and do things. Start taking care of life. After forty days, you need to start finding your new life without your spouse. This all varies greatly between men and women.

Jewish mourning is broken into four stages:

ANINUT. This refers to the time. Of death. In the time of burial. Anywhere from 24 to 48 hours.

SHIVA. This is a seven-day following the burial of your loved one. This would be a time of deep warning. And remembering.

SHLOSHIM. This is the next 30 days we're mourning continues and life starts to get back to normal.

THE FIRST YEAR. This is observed by family. "With times of remembering". (Reference: Jacksonville. Jewish funerals. "Defining the Stages of Jewish Mourning" Internet.)

Chapter 11
ACEDIA

THE BLUES, IN A FOG, THE FUNK, DEPRESSION

a-ce-di-a spiritual or mental sloth or apathy.
(Oxford Languages)

Acedia is the condition or state of mind a person has before depression. For some, depression may never come. Acedia describes the condition where the person can't get out of their own way. Other ways to describe this are listlessness, not caring, melancholy, the blues, apathy, tedium, boredom, lack of interest, and the blahs. The person doesn't want to do anything. They feel like they are in funk. The things that used to interest them or excite them no longer do.

In the fifth century, John Cassian a monks noticed that they were susceptible to acedia. They referred to it as a demon that needed to be cast out. For me, the place to start looking is to ask, "Holy Spirit, what is going on here? How do we pray?" Whenever a demon could be involved, I begin the prayer time with the following: "In the name of Jesus, we bind any satanic power in or around or about this person. We command you to go." It is important to begin the conversation by asking them to describe their condition and asking them to put language to it; for example, "I feel like I got the blahs." In that case, we pray, "In the name of Jesus, blahs go. Be gone. Acedia, go. Be gone in the name of Jesus."

In today's world, we can anesthetize ourselves by being online, on social media, playing a game, or watching

TV. I fall into these traps way too often. Is it demonic, or is it a choice that I make? I'm not one who tends to see demonic activity in every circumstance. I don't believe the demons went away just because we don't recognize them in our culture. We often view the devil and his minions as a fairy tale, something that was happening back when Jesus was walking the earth, but we don't see it now. Bull puckey! We are influenced by demons probably every day, but we have been so desensitized that we don't know it. Here are some examples. (The source internet The conversation Acedia and Wikipedia Acedia)

Have you ever had malicious thoughts about someone you know? "Betty Lou hates me."

Driving down the road, have you ever thought about running your vehicle into a group of people?

Driving over a bridge, have you ever thought, "Many people have jumped off this bridge. It sure would be easy to get out of all my troubles. Just stop the car and take a look. It would be easy."

Have you ever lustfully looked at a person of the opposite sex and thought "Hmmm. What a good job God has done with her or him," or "WOW! Girl in tight red sweater," or "WOW! Guy in tight red sweater"?

These unholy thoughts may be from an outside source, or they could be just your old sin nature rising to the top every now and then.

Chapter 12
DEALING WITH LONELINESS

I lived with my parents until I left to go to college and then I had roommates. After school, I moved back into my parents' home, and then I moved in with my wife. I have never been alone until that day I came home from the hospital after Kate died. Now what? At first, I tried to keep myself busy. One day I sat down and had a talk with myself and Holy Spirit. The conclusion was I needed to become comfortable being alone. I asked Holy Spirit, "How do I do that?" I received no big revelation. I noticed when I was lonely if I put worship music on and sang along, the loneliness would lift.

I observed the people around me. One friend spent hours working out. He looked great, but he didn't like being with himself. Another had the life ambition of watching all the movies she could find for free. And then there was my friend who went looking for love. And boy did she find it. There are both male and female predators out there. Be careful. How are you doing? Does loneliness creep up on you?

Here is how I become comfortable with the hush. I started slowly being in the kitchen without any background noise. Then I worked up to sitting in a room by myself. No noise. The first couple of times, I fell into the pit of remorse. And sometimes it was creepy. Then one day, I invited Holy Spirit to come sit with me. No talking, just silence. Then I asked the question, "How can I lead a productive life?"

For me, that's making something with my hands. I don't know how you will work it out. Try asking Holy Spirit to show you. Most people want an experience like Saul's blinding light. They want the audible voice of God. The odds are that is not going to happen. It might be that you need to just do something, and then you will find it. Every journey begins with the first step. Dealing with loneness will be the special plan Holy Spirit has planned for you.

Keep in mind you are a delight in the Lord's eyes. He is eagerly waiting to hear from you. I remember the day one of our grandchildren was moving back to Florida. The anticipation and excitement of them coming back home to live was great. Kate had a mobile app to track your friends, and we used it to watch their progress as they drove from Missouri.

"The Lord makes firm the steps of the one who delights in him" (Psalm 37:23).

The God of all creation is watching closely, like he is walking by your side. He delights to see how you are going to work out this challenge with the help of Holy Spirit. Are you going to ask for help? Or are you going to do it in your own strength?

"The heart of man plans his ways, but the Lord establishes his steps." Proverbs 16:9.

We make plans, hopefully prayerfully with Holy Spirit. Doing it this way, Father God can direct our steps. One day, long ago, I was minding my own business when Holy Spirit interrupted me. He showed me, in my mind's eye, a straight line and said, "This is my good, pleasing, and perfect will for you." On top of the perfect-will line, he laid my walk: a red line that went above and below the perfect will line. Sometimes my walk and the perfect plan line were the same, and sometimes my walk line was above or below. Holy Spirit said, "As long as you are seeking me, I will get you back on track to complete the assignment I gave you."

Let's look at your soul. How is your soul? Your soul is your mind, your will, and your emotions. One of the reasons I wrote this book is I want people to be emotionally sound, leading a whole and healthy life. A close friend asked me, "How is your soul doing through all of this?" I responded that my mind and my thoughts were running all over the place, out of control. My will was being as willful as it can be. And my emotions were like Disney World's Space Mountain roller coaster before they slowed it down. That pretty much sums up the first six months of my big adventure of being a widower.

Pray this prayer: *"Loving, kind, and compassionate Father God, help me to get a grip on my thoughts, my will, and my emotions. Help me to see my world the way you do. Keep me in the circle of your love and put a hedge of protection around me in Jesus' name."*

> *"Do not conform to the pattern of this world, but be transformed by the renewing of your mind. Then you will be able to test and approve what God's will is – his good, pleasing and perfect will"* *Romans 12:2. (NIV)*

Chapter 13
FEAR ANXIETY WORRY

Fear is a big one. Fear is usually accompanied by his gangster brother, anxiety, who causes you to worry. They work hand-in-hand to mess with your head. The enemy will use fear to keep you from being healed. Fear and anxiety are very invasive; they can overtake you at any time. Like a vacuum, fear and anxiety will suck up the important things in your life. The time and the energy expended on worrying won't leave you with any time left to live life. Worrying is meditating on fear, and anxiety's steals your faith. The devil will lie to you. He is the father of lies. Every time I had time to think, in those first six months, I was inundated with fear and anxiety. Fear that I would lose the house. Worry that a bill wouldn't get paid. Anxious about letting family down. It's getting ugly; I'll stop. Get your own stuff to worry about. (I'm teasing of course. Human beings tend to have many fears and worries in common.)

*"There is **No Fear** in love, but perfect love casts out **fear**" 1John 4:18a*

*"**Rejoice** in the Lord always. I will say it again: **REJOICE!** 6 Be anxious for nothing, but in everything, by prayer and supplication with **Thanksgiving**, let your request be made known to God. 7 and the **peace** of God, which surpasses all comprehension, will guard your hearts and your minds in Christ Jesus. Philippians 4:4,6-7 (NASB95) (Emphasis added)*

44

Chapter 14
FINDING PEACE

How do you find the PEACE of GOD?

For me, finding the peace of God starts with finding a quiet place and dialing down. I focus on Jesus being right there with me. I take a few slow, deep breaths and let all the anxiety and fear leave with each consecutive breath. This is a relaxation technique. With each exhale, you relax your body just a little more with each breath. I do this while speaking quietly, "Fear, worry, and anxiety, go. Be gone." Now that I'm with Jesus, and I've quieted my inner being (that voice in my head), I bring up a love verse I have memorized.

> See how great a love the Father has bestowed on us, that we would be called children of God; and such we are." 1 John 3:1 (NASB95)

> "God so loved me that he gave His one and only son that if I believe in him I will not perish but have eternal life" (John 3:16, adapted to first person)

The secret is to say the verses out loud. Why? Because the self-talk stops when you're talking out loud. Not many thoughts can break through when you're talking. Another advantage to speaking it is that, somehow, the words get into your spirit, your inner being.

On Kate's third day in the hospital, I received Psalms 34 from the Lord. Any time I was gripped by fear, I would read the whole thing, most of the time out loud. These verses were particularly helpful. Read the whole psalm.

Psalms 34:4, 6, 15, 19 (NASB95, emphasis added):

*4 I sought the Lord, and he answered me; he delivered me from all my **fears**.*
*6 This poor man called, and the Lord heard him and saved him out of **all his troubles**; I called and Jesus heard **me** and saved **me** out of all **my** troubles.*
*15 The eyes of the Lord are toward the righteous his **ear attentive to their cry**;*
*19 Many are the **afflictions** of the righteous, but the Lord delivers them from them **all**; I have many troubles, but Holy Spirit delivers **me** from them all.*

*1 John 4:18-19 "There is **No Fear** in love; but perfect love casts out **fear**, because fear involves punishment. And the one who **fears** is not made perfect in love. We love because he first loved us." NASB95 (emphasis added)*

I walk in *love*. Jesus, who is perfect love, drives out all my fears. I love, or I am *loved*, because he first loved me.

*Psalms 27:1-3 "The Lord is my light and my Salvation-**whom shall I fear**? The Lord is the stronghold of my life – of **whom shall I be fear?** The Lord is the stronghold of my life. - of whom shall I be afraid? When the wicked advance against me to devour me, it is my enemies and my foes who will stumble and fall. Though an army besiege me, my heart **will not fear**; though war break out against me, even then I will be confident" (NIV, emphasis added)*

*Psalms 23:4: "Even though I walk through the darkest valley, I **will fear no evil,** <u>for you are with me</u>; your rod and your staff, they comfort me" (NIV, emphasis added).*

*Psalms 91:5-6: "**You will not fear** the terror of night, nor the arrow that flies by day, 6 nor the pestilence that stalks in the darkness, nor the plague that destroys at midday." (NIV, emphasis added).*

*Psalms 112:6-8: "Surely the righteous will never be shaken; they will be remembered forever. They will have **No Fear** of bad news; their hearts are steadfast, <u>trusting in the Lord. Their hearts are secure</u>, they will have **No Fear**; in the end they will look in triumph on their foes" (NIV, emphasis added).*

*Isa 41:10: "So do **not fear**, for <u>I am with you</u>; do not be dismayed, for I am your God. I will strengthen you and <u>help you</u>; I will uphold you with my righteous right hand" (NIV, emphasis added).*

Pray this prayer: *Father God, creator of heaven and earth, you are the King of Kings and the Lord of Lords. You are the awesome, almighty God. I come before you in the name of Jesus. Fear has no hold over me. I refuse to fear. I will not act impulsively because of urgency. Help, Lord. Help me to see what I can do now. I turn everything over to you. I am blessed coming in and blessed going out. Everything I put my hand to is blessed. I know it, and you know it. Thank you, Jesus. Come, Holy Spirit.*

I've found that memorization is difficult, so I decided I wasn't going to memorize anything. I carried verses on 3 by 5" cards and pulled them out as needed. I found that after carrying a 3 x 5" card for a week or two, I had the verse memorized. There wasn't any effort on my part to consciously memorize it. I just kept reading them repeatedly, at stop lights, bathroom breaks, or waiting, and sometimes I would set a goal to read them every hour on the hour.

One year our daughter wanted to go on a band trip to Europe. We agreed, but first we required her to memorize Psalms 91. How do you expect that was received? Tell a 17-year-old she needs to memorize sixteen verses and see how it goes for you. And of course, she asked the question, "*Why*?" "Because I said so," I answered. Again she asked, "Why?" I said, "Because your life depends on it." Psalms 91 was taped in front of every seat in the car, on the kitchen table, next to the TV, and at every seat watching the TV. It was taped to the bathroom mirror and was next to her bed. Before we started the car, before dinner, and during commercials, we'd all read Psalms 91 out loud.

Why? Because our lives depend on it. Years went by, and she was married and expecting a baby. A tornado was reported in her area. She began to pray and recite Psalms 91. Time passed, and there was a knock on the door, not just a knock, an urgent banging. It was her in-laws. They came to see if she was still alive because the tornado went through the condos where they were living. The row of condos that she lived in were still standing, and the other condos had their second floors blown away. I wonder if Psalms 91 had anything to do with it.

More years went by. Her two children became young adults and were now in their late teens. A tornado was reported in the area. They grabbed the mattress off a bed and pulled it over them in the bathtub. There aren't any cellars in Florida were we live. In the tub, they prayed and recited Psalms 91. The wind stopped blowing. They later learned that the tornado came up behind the row of houses and took out the backyards. The houses were untouched. I wonder if Psalms 91 had anything to do with that.

Psalms 91 is painted on our living room floor under the rug. The rest of the house is covered with many other scripture verses. Why?

> *"For the word of God is alive and active. and sharper than any double-edged sword."*
> *Hebrews 4:12a (NASB95*

> *"No weapon forged against you will prevail, and you will refute every tongue that accuses you."*
> *Isaiah 54:17a (NIV)*

> *"Then Satan answered the Lord and said, 'Does Job fear God for nothing? Have you not put a hedge (of protection) around him and his house and all he has, on every side? You have blessed the work of his hands, and his possessions have increased in the land.'" Job 1:9-10*

Keep in mind that when fear, anxiety, and worry are breaking down the door, the only thing to do is run to Father God. He is our ever-present help in times of danger.

"The Lord is a stronghold for the oppressed, a stronghold in times of trouble" Psalms 9:9 ESV

"The salvation of the righteous is from the Lord; he is their stronghold in times of trouble" Psalms 37:39

The challenge is to learn to run to Jesus immediately. It's hard because we think we are just hearing our own self-talk. It could be that, but more than likely, the negative stuff is coming from a demon assigned to make your life suck. Remember*: "He has given his angels charge concerning YOU to guard YOU in all YOUR ways." Psalms 91:11 (NASB95)*

This is where we get our guardian angels, more than one. My experience is that they are always working on our behalf. But for some reason, they go on high alert when we pray, and they really jump in when we pray the Word.

"Praise the Lord, you his angels, Mighty in strength who perform (obey (who hearken to) His word, Obeying the voice of His word. Psalms 103:2 (NASB95)

The idea I see here is that the angels are waiting to hear us speak God's Word in a particular situation so that they can move into high gear. Demons, on the other hand, flee when we start quoting, speaking out loud, shouting at the top of our lungs, or reading, Daddy God's Word.

Pray this prayer: *"Father God, who blesses me with every spiritual blessing, help me to distinguish between your voice and the voice of the evil one in Jesus' name."*

Chapter 15
WHO IS THE DEVIL?

I feel that I'm being prompted to add this section on the devil: Lucifer, slew foot, Satan, the enemy, the liar, the deceiver, the accuser, the dark shadow, the thief. Every culture on earth gives many words to the things that affect them. I believe that the Alaskan natives have 27 different words for snow.

In America today I have heard that there was a study done asking the question is the devil real. Only 51%of American Christians believe in a living and real Satan. Bad things just happen to all of us. And some bad things happen because your enemy, the devil, is messing with you. Angles are working on our behalf preventing the devil from messing with us. The Barna Group study reported in Faith and Christianity

> *"The thief comes only to steal and kill and destroy; I have come that they may have life, and have it abundantly." (John 10:10,* Jesus speaking).

> *"God opposes the proud but gives grace to the humble. Submit yourselves, therefore, to God. Resist the devil, and he will flee from you. Draw near to God and he will draw near to you."*
> James 4:6-8

I believe that when you became a follower of Jesus, you joined a war, whether or not you wanted to. Before you were a believer, the devil barely noticed you. Why should he have given you any attention when you were already working for him? Then you became a follower of Jesus. Now the devil is very concerned about you because every time you pray, you mess up his plans. Every prayer you pray is "spiritual warfare," because every prayer interrupts the devil's plans. So here we are in a battle we never wanted, in a fight no one told us about when we signed up.

"The weapons we fight with are not the weapons of the world. On the contrary, they have divine power to demolish strongholds. We demolish arguments and every pretension that sets itself up against the knowledge of God, and we take captive every thought to make it obedient to Christ" 2 Corinthians 10:4-5 (NIV)

How do we break the power, the strongholds of the enemy? We pray. Prayer is one of the strongest weapons in the world. Prayer can change nations, and it can certainly change a wayward child. I have seen prayer do both. I have also seen prayers of a mother go unanswered. I have no idea why, other than that the prayer wasn't God's plan for that person at this point in time. If you have a wild child, the two prayers to pray are in Ephesians 1:17-21 and Ephesians 3:16-19. Insert their name in place of "you."

"I heard a loud voice in heaven saying, 'Now the salvation, and the power, and the Kingdom of our God, and the authority of his Christ have come, for the accuser of our brothers has been thrown down, who accuses them day and night before our God. And they have conquered him by the blood of the lamb, and by the word of their testimony, for they love. Not their lives, even unto death.'" (Revelation 12:10-11)

The accuser of the brothers has been cast out of heaven. He still accuses us of every little sin, such as every word that was spoken in anger, even though they're covered by the blood of Jesus. The blood of Jesus is one of the strongest weapons we have. We received this from Jesus when he died on the cross and rose from the dead, so that we can come before God without being accused. Another weapon we have is our testimony. Our testimony includes how we accepted Jesus, what happened, and how we responded. The testimony of what happened to us after we made Jesus Lord of our lives is very strong weapons to fight off the enemy. Every time you tell somebody how it was and what God did, it gives the devil a black eye, figuratively.

For instance, the devil tried to kill me. I was out riding my bike and somehow, I fell off and the bike was destroyed. I probably had an accident with a car or something else; I'm not sure because I don't remember. Somehow, I made it home and called my wife, asking her when she was coming home. She realized that something was completely off because I had lost about 20 years of memory. I was asking questions that would have been relevant 20 years ago but were completely off now. She called our daughter who came over to the house, saw that I was a bloody, banged-up mess, and called the ambulance.

When we got to the hospital, they took x-rays, and the doctor called Kate into his office for a consultation. He said there is no way I should have been walking; there's no way I should have been talking, even in incoherent sentences. He showed her the x-ray, and the back half of the brain was black. The doctor said if he didn't know I was in an accident, he would say I had a massive stroke. The doctor told them that he did not expect me to make it through the night because of this massive brain trauma.

I did make it through the night, and the next day, when they did the MRI, they couldn't find anything wrong. After four days in the ICU, I came back to somewhat normal. Most of my memory returned, except for about four years. I still don't remember what happened that day. All I know is that the church came together and prayed, and I made it through a massive brain trauma. Prayer does work. Father God does heal his children. You see how that testimony gives credence that God does heal, God does love us, and God has a plan for our lives. Obviously, the plan for my life was not over at that point in time.

Who is the devil? The devil is a created being. He was created with the angels. In the heavenly ranking, we have God, Jesus, and Holy Spirit on the top rank, and then come the angels. The devil is in no way equal with Lord God Almighty or Jesus or Holy Spirit. The devil is not Jesus' brother. When the devil was kicked out of heaven, a third of the angels went with him, and they are lesser in power. That third now make up the demons that roam the earth (Revelation 12:4).

God versus Satan

1. God, Jesus, and Holy Spirit are eternal, with no beginning no end. God, Jesus and Holy Spirit are one and the same. Jesus is fully God and fully Holy Spirit. Holy Spirit is fully Jesus and fully God.

The devil was created by God. The devil was an angel. Angels are created beings. When you die, you don't become an Angel. You become a spirit being who rules and reigns with Jesus.

When I was young in the Lord, someone tried to explain the Trinity to me; Father, Son, and Holy Spirit are one and the same. It wasn't working for me, so I asked my pastor, "What is this thing called the Trinity?" He laughed and said, "That's a hard one to get your head wrapped around." Look at it this way: God is the Father, Jesus is the son and your brother, and the Holy Spirit is what ties you, the Father, and Jesus all together. Picture a triangle, and at one point is Jesus, the next point is the Father, and you are at the last point. The Holy Spirit is the triangle that connects all of you together.

2. God is mercy, grace, love, patience, and kindness. The devil saw this as weakness.
The devil thought he could overthrow God. Pride, selfish ambition, and arrogance are in the devil's make-up.

3. God is light. Father God is the giver of light.

The devil is darkness. The devil is the counterfeit of light. The lie is that the guru, the ascended master, the yogi, the buddha and the fortune teller are where you can find light. For the follower of Jesus, these options will dim Jesus' light in you.

4. God has the Kingdom of God—a kingdom.

The devil has an empire that he acquired when Adam and Eve gave it up to him.

5. Father God has a plan for our salvation. His plan is to give us life by bringing us into his kingdom.

The devil wants to steal, kill, and destroy life and steal our salvation, keeping us out of the Kingdom of God. The devil will lie to us, telling us not to give up the things of the world—the things of his realm.

6. God is omniscient—*all knowing.* Before the beginning of time, God knew it all. The devil does not know what the future is.

The devil can manipulate the present. Manipulation is being able to whisper in somebody's ear and them to act on it. For example, imagine a fortune teller says you are going to meet a tall, dark stranger. Then you go to the coffee shop and sit down, when in walks a tall, dark stranger. Driving by the coffee shop, the stranger had a sudden urge for coffee: "Coffee. I need coffeeeee." He is being manipulated a demon. The only seat left in the place is at your table.

How do we know the devil is not all-knowing? He would not have rebelled. He would have known what was coming. He would have seen the boot hitting his butt kicking him out of heaven.

7. God is omnipresent—*everywhere all at the same time.*

The devil works in the present only. How do we know the devil is not omnipresent? He got kicked out of heaven. He is no longer present in heaven. He's not everywhere all at the same time and never has been.

8. God is omnipotent—*all powerful.* He has more power than any created being.

The devil is limited in power. How do we know? God kicked Satan out. God, the greater power, kicked out the devil, the lesser power.

9. God, by grace, gives people spiritual gifts to build up the church.

The devil gives the illusion of power by works. The devil is a counterfeiter.

10. God is creative. He created all things, and all things are held together by him.

The devil is not creative. At best, he is a manipulator and counterfeiter. He can sometimes fool us by making things look like he created them.

Chapter 16
HOW TO PRAY

This next section teaches how to pray. Some of us might need a refresher on the basics of prayer. Can we talk?

Prayer is one of the simplest things a Christian does. It is also one of the hardest. Why? Because we have to get our heads wrapped around the idea that *"The prayer of a righteous man [or woman, that's us] is powerful and effective." James 5:16 (NIV)*

We don't see ourselves as mighty pray-ers. We pray, but we don't see it happening in our mind's eye. "God is watching from a distance" we think. "God doesn't really care about little old me." NO. He's right there, waiting for you to have a conversation with him. He is in you. He will never leave you. He will not leave you without his help. For some reason, Father God wants to hear from us a lot. He loves you just the way you are.

Pray this prayer: *Lord Jesus, help quiet all the voices and thoughts that are not mine. I want to hear you and you alone. Give me ears to hear, eyes to see, and a nose to smell the difference between you and the evil one.*

Yes, smell; sometimes, though not often, you can smell a demon. For me, Jesus has his own fragrance, something like lilacs.

One of the key concepts of prayer is that Jesus has opened the door for us to speak directly to the Lord God Almighty.

"Jesus said to him, 'I am the way, and the truth, and the life. No one comes to the Father except through me.'" John 14:6

"Jesus said, "You may ask me for anything in my name and I will do it.'" John 14:14.

"Let us then approach God's throne of grace with confidence, so that we may receive mercy and find grace to help us in our time of need." Hebrews 4:16.

I usually start praying by saying, "Father God, I come before you in the name of Jesus." Some people tack it on the end, saying "in Jesus' name we pray" (John 14:13-14). Many things happened on the cross, and one of those things is our ability to come boldly before the throne of God. This promise is almost too great to comprehend; if we ask anything in the name of Jesus, he will do it. Keep in mind that it must be according to his will (1 John 5:14-15). This privilege is not to be used lightly or flippantly. The world has been changed throughout history by people praying in the name of Jesus.

Hitler and the German army. rolled over France, Pushing the allied armies.to the sea. It appeared that two thirds of the Allied forces would be killed or captured. On the 23rd of May. King George VI Called for a National Day of Prayer. That Sunday, the churches were packed. The Nation of Britain prayed. for deliverance. The churches and cathedrals were so full. that people were standing outside. The next day. an urgent call and out. for 800 vessels. to cross the English Channel. and the rescue the troops. The mission was accomplished 335,000 were rescued. The

German army missed the chance to destroy England. Christianity How a day of prayer saved Britain at Dunkirk. By Reverend Cannon J John. 20 July 2017.

During World War II, The BBC asked the people of the England to pray at 9 pm for the nation. when Big Ben struck 9. They called it the silent minute.

A German officer being interrogated after the war. Was asked why. Germany lost the war. He said because you had a secret weapon that we could not figure out. But it was very powerful. Because the people of England prayed. God moved to protect his children. He has given us a way to invite him into every situation. Ref. Margo Lestz, "Big Ben Silent Minute."

One warm summer evening, Kate and I had come off route 81 in Pennsylvania and turned onto 61 heading into Pottsville. From 81 all the way to the city limits, the road is going down the mountain. Along the road are several places for a runaway truck pull off. It's a four-lane highway, but at the bottom, it narrows into two lanes where the road goes under a railroad. There was a bit of water lying in the bottom of the underpass, and in front of us. Two cars were moving slowly through the water. About 300 yards from the underpass, I noticed an 18-wheeler coming very fast down the mountain behind us. We were all about to die. I prayed, "Help Jesus. Help in the name of Jesus. Help, Jesus." I also prayed in the spirit.

The trucker passed us in the underpass. His truck tipped on its left wheels and scraped the top of the tunnel, pouring down a shower of sparks. The underpass prevented the truck from turning over completely. Somehow, we all came out the other side alive. His trailer was a little beat up, and his brakes were on fire. When I got through, I pulled up behind him to see if I could help in any way. He was foaming down his burning brakes with a fire extinguisher. He said he was carrying swinging beef and when the beef rock the truck went up on its side.

Mark 11:22-24 is one of the foundational verses on the concept of prayer, asking and believing. These verses have some great promises. Remember, Jesus was fully man and had all the challenges and highs and lows we have. Who of us have ever thought, "Jesus doesn't know what I'm going through"? That's how we feel from time to time. we do have my moments of great faith, but then there are those other times.

> *And Jesus answered. "Have faith in God," "Truly I tell you, whoever <u>says </u>to this mountain, 'Be taken up and cast into the sea,' and **does not doubt in his heart** but **believes** that what he <u>say </u>will happen, it will be granted to him. Therefore I tell you, all things for which you pray and <u>ask</u>, **believe** that you have received them, and they will be granted you." Mark 11:22-24*

Here are a few things we need to look at.

1. Have a faith that rests on God. To do this, we must believe that God is interested in us and wants to hear from us. Have a trust in God to take care of all our situations, troubles, broken heart, and disasters. Father God, the Lord God Almighty, creator of heaven and earth, sent his son Jesus to earth so that we could have easy access to him. *Wow*!

2. Notice the words "says," "say," and "ask": "*if anyone says...believes that what they say will happen...whatever you ask for.*" This may be a different concept, but we need to talk to things. Jesus did. Look at Matthew chapters eight through ten. Jesus commanded sick people to do things. Remember the wind and the waves? Jesus commanded them to be still.

> "*He got up, rebuked the wind and said to the waves, "Quiet be still!" Then wind died down and it was completely calm*" (*Matt 8:23-27; Mark 4:39*).

We can't rebuke something by thinking it. We need to talk to it. We need to talk to the challenges in our lives. Pray this prayer: "*Father, I was whole a little while ago, and now I'm not. I need to be whole again. Body, soul (my mind, my will, and my emotions), and spirit in me, be whole. Holy Spirit, come heal me. Holy Spirit, make me whole now in Jesus' name.*"

If we have a bill we cannot pay, pray like this: "Father God, I just got this bill, and I have no idea how to pay it. Bill, in the name of Jesus be paid. Money, come to me now. Help, Lord Jesus. Help."

When praying for someone's healing, talk to the part that needs healing: "Kidneys, be healed; work right. Infection, go in the name of Jesus."

We can pray like this for yourself too: "Viruses and bad bacteria, parasites, fungus and molds, die. Be gone. Body, be healed. My body is healed."

The day after Kate went into the hospital, the roofers came and put a new roof on the house. Kate told me the money was there to pay for it. I couldn't find the money; it wasn't in the checking account. I prayed, "O God, O God, O God, help." I called the roofer to explain the situation; he said, "Pay me when you can." I started paying it off in $100 chunks, then a $1000 chunk, then several large chunks. I was talking to the bill the whole time: "Bill, be paid. Money, come to me now. Money, I summon you. I hereby call you to appear to pay off this bill. Help me, Lord Jesus."

Most of us are already talking to inanimate objects and to people who can't hear us. Take, for instance, sitting at traffic lights: "Come on change." Consider our reaction to people in other cars: "You idiot! Get out of the way. Use your turn signal %&^$@."

We need to start talking to ourselves *out loud: "*I can get through this. I Will Survive. Jesus loves me; this I know for the Bible tells me so". (See John 3:16.)

Here is a good prayer: *"Holy Spirit, come now. Give me wisdom, stature, and great favor with all the people I'm dealing with in Jesus' name"* (Psalm 5:12, Luke 2:52).

We sometimes wonder why we have so many negative thoughts, such as "No one likes me. My life is over. I can't make it"? Could it be that those thoughts are coming from an outside source? We are probably hearing from a demon whose assignment is to make sure we don't come out whole and healthy on the other side of our situation. The devil wants to take us out of the game. (If this is scary, remember where I contrast God and the devil.) The only way to fight back is to tell the devil what Jesus says about us. Take a breath and ask the question, "Is that a Jesus thought, a demon thought, or my thought?" What is my self-talk saying?

Are we hearing things that are negative and agreeing with them?

Pray this prayer: *"In Jesus' name, I bind any satanic power in, around, or about me, and I command it to go. Be gone. I take every thought captive and make it obedient to Christ (2 Corinthians 10:5). Help me, Jesus. Help, Jesus."*

In the appendix, there is a list describing whom Jesus says you are. Its title is "Who Am I." Pick three or four of them, and work on them throughout the day. Here are three to get you started.

> 1. *In me there is no darkness. I have been purified. All my sins are forgiven.*
>
> *"This is the message we have heard from him and declare to you: God is light; in him there is no darkness at all." 1 John 1:5 (NIV)*
>
> *"But if we walk in the light… the blood of Jesus, his son, cleanses from all sin."*
> *1 John 1:7 (NASB95)*
>
> 2. *Father God loves me. I am his favorite child.*
>
> *"See what great a love the Father has bestowed (lavished0 on us, that we would be called children of God! And such we are."*
> *1 John 3:1 NASB95.*

If this is hard to say, it's because we don't believe it. Shout it five or six times, as if our baseball team just made a homerun: "I am his favorite child." This came from two places. The first was a sermon by Janet

Randall, a former missionary, that we are God's *favorites*, as if that is our tribe, like the Hittites, Kohathites, and Levites. The second is from me telling my grandchildren that the closest one to me, at that moment, is my favorite. One day, the youngest heard me tell the older one that he is my favorite. "How come!" the youngest asked, "I'm your favorite and he is your favorite?" The explanation was simple. When God looks around and sees all his children, he sees them all, and each one of them is his favorite. When Father God looks around, he sees all his children equally. No one person is better than the other. He is delighted with each of us who abide in him, rest in him, want to do what he is doing. Father God looks at the bag lady walking down the street, who is a little crazy, and your pastor, who seems sane, as equals. Through Jesus, our Father God sees us all the same. We can't make Father God any happier with us, and we can't get more saved, than the day we first prayed the prayer becoming his child.

3. *I refuse to fear. I will not be afraid. Father God's perfect love drives out all fear.*

"There is No Fear in love, but perfect love casts out fear, because fear has to do with punishment and whoever fears is not made perfect in love." *1 John 4:18*

BELIEVE

The backbone of prayer is believing that Lord God Almighty, creator of heaven and Earth, has heard our prayer and wants to move on our behalf. How do we do that? For the most part we believe, believe, believe, waver, believe, doubt, then believe again. Over the years, and in the moment we prayed, we were believing it was going to happen. But as time goes on, our believing begins to waver. Along come those thoughts, out of nowhere, that probably aren't our thoughts. These thoughts try to steal our believing. If we accept them, we are agreeing with the enemy. If we start praising God with our lips, actually saying it out loud, those thoughts go away.

Pray this prayer: *"Thank you, Jesus that you love me. Thank you, Jesus, you want to meet my needs. You are the King of kings and the Lord of lords. You are the Holy and Anointed One. Blessed be the name of the Lord Jesus Christ, the alpha and omega, the beginning of everything and the end of everything, my ever-present help in danger, in fear, and when I hurt. I am victorious, I win when it's all said and done."*

Listening is a key part of praying: *"Because he loves me,"* says the Lord, *"I will rescue him; I will protect him, for he acknowledges my name, **he will call on me, and I will answer him**; I will be with him in trouble, I will deliver him and honor him."* Psalm 91:14-15 (NIV)

Bible verses need to be converted into first person. It is a confession; we are talking to Father God. We are telling Father God what he told us:

*Because I love the Lord, Jesus will rescue me; he will protect me, because I acknowledge His name, **I will call upon Jesus and he will answer me** (I can't hear the answer if I'm not listening); he will be with me in trouble, he will deliver me and honor me. With a long life he will satisfy me and show me His Salvation.*

Suppose we had a friend, and we did all the talking. This friend couldn't get a word in. How long do we think they would be our friend? They probably would have realized early in the relationship that "this ain't gonna work."

Prayer is a two-way conversation. Prayer is what brings us into relationship with Father God. Holy Spirit wants us to shut up, be still, and listen to that wee small voice inside our heads. That's Holy Spirit. Ask the Father what we should pray for or how we should pray, and Holy Spirit will lead you.

"But when he, the Spirit of Truth, comes, He will guide you into all truth; for He will not speak on his own initiative, but whatever He hears, He will speak; and He will disclose to you what is to come." John 16: 13

Holy Spirit is capable of breaking through all the noise. Our spirit knows the voice of Holy Spirit. Keep in mind that the Holy Spirit's voice sounds like your self-talk in your head. Sometimes we will have thoughts that are beyond our ability to think or know.

"When he has brought out all his own, he goes ahead of them, and his sheep follow him because they know his voice." John 10:4 (NASB95)

The devil wants to harm us. Sometimes, he will tell you, "This isn't going to work." His voice in our head tells us negative garbage and brings up our past: "Remember third grade and how you messed _____ up?" "I'm not very good at this." When this happens, quietly start to praise Father God out loud. The devil will flee because; he really doesn't like to hear people praising God. *"Submit yourselves, then, to God. Resist the devil, and he will flee from you. Come near to God and he will come near to you." James 4:7-8*

Praise is one of the quickest ways to resist the devil
and come near to God.

The devil's voice is sometimes harsh and abrasive and
other times its as sweet as honey. He doesn't love you.
His words cause confusion and are filled with lies and
distrust. The devil's words will wound us rather than
bring joy and peace into our heart. He never calls us
daughter or son; he starts immediately into what he has
to say. Most of the time, when we hear demons
speaking, it sounds like our own thoughts, but they are
negative. Sometimes, we will have a thought float
through our mind that is trying to get me into trouble:
"You can go over there. It's okay; they'll never find out."
The devil is a liar and a seducer. His seductions are
always sweet and appealing and in the end we will be
messed up.

God's voice is calm and usually calls us by name or as
his beloved son or daughter. He never tells us to do
something that would contradict his Word, nor anything
that would be against the law. He will not contradict
what we know is right. His voice is always loving, kind,
and compassionate. Even when he's telling us to "Stop
it." Listening takes practice; don't be afraid. God never
brings up our mess-ups from the past. He never brings
up our past sins because, in heaven, they never
happened. Father God is all about the possibilities. In
heaven there are only possibilities. He doesn't
remember our sins or even know that they happen.
Holy Spirit is our cheerleader. You can do it. Fight;
Fight. Never give up. Dig deep; you got this. He is all
about the future. Holy Spirit is all about future success.
The enemy may slip something in, but we will know it.
Our spirit is in connection with Holy Spirit, and we will
be able to separate the two voices. It may take a little

practice, but it will happen. When we really need to hear from Holy Spirit, it's good play worship music to change the atmosphere. Worship and praise music is continually happening in heaven.

Here's a story I heard. It's one of those stories that cannot be proven. I usually don't tell these stories because they seem unrealistic.

God told this young lad to go to Ireland. When he got there, he asked, "Now what?" He believes he heard Holy Spirit say to go to a certain corner where there is a church; then to go inside and ask how he can help. He found the street, and found the corner, and there was a church. He went inside and asked the priest, "How can I help?" The priest told him they were painting the whole inside of the building and needed help. He told the priest his story.

He stayed there for a couple of months, and while he painted, he prayed for Ireland, the Irish, and this church. He noticed that his negative thoughts were becoming overbearing. He started to pray about the negative thoughts. He realized that he was being tormented by demons, which had been hanging around this church.

One night, while in his little room that had a bed, a chair, and a couple of cardboard boxes, Holy Spirit told him, "Pray a prayer to seal the room off from the rest of the church and not allow anything to leave." He did that. Then he heard the Lord say, "Turn on your worship music." He did that.

Then the Lord gave him the ability to see the demons that had been tormenting him. For some reason, they couldn't leave the room because he had sealed it with prayer, and they were now being tormented by the worship music. And this struck him as one of the funniest things he had ever seen. During his remaining time in Ireland in that church, whenever he felt negative thoughts coming on, he would start to laugh, and they would leave instantly.

Praise keeps faith alive. We praise God for what he has done in the Bible, for what he has done in our past, and for what he is about to do. Praise keeps the door to heaven open. We praise him even if we haven't seen what He's about to do. We praise him even when we don't feel like it, especially when we don't feel like it. It's an act of our will. Praise needs to become a way of life. I exist; therefore, I will praise Father God. I am praise.

> *"Rejoice always, pray without ceasing, in*
> *everything give thanks; for this is God's will for*
> *you in Christ Jesus."*
> *1 Thessalonians 5:16-18 (NASB95).*

> *"Rejoice in the Lord always. Again I will say*
> *Rejoice! Let your gentle spirit be known to all.*
> *The Lord is near. Be anxious for nothing, but in*
> *everything by prayer and supplication, with*
> *thanksgiving, let your requests be made known*
> *to God. And the peace of God, which surpasses*
> *all comprehension, will guard your hearts and*
> *your minds in Christ Jesus."*
> *Philippians 4:4-7 (NASB95).*

Here's something to try when we need to know an answer. When we need to know what to do. Before we go to bed, pray a simple little prayer:

"Come, Holy Spirit. Speak to me tonight in dreams and visions, so when I wake up, I will know the answer."

It is surprising how many times Holy Spirit has come through with an answer. Sometimes, we just wake up knowing the answer without knowing how we got it. It works. Don't know how It works; it just does. And if it doesn't work, so what? It didn't cost us anything. It is just a tool. The answer is coming. Jesus always comes through. Keep on trying. Never give up. (See Luke 18:1).

Have you ever heard the phrase, "I'd like to sleep on it"? I believe the origin is with the Society of Friends, "The Quakers." The idea is that sleeping on a question, a problem, or a decision gives time for God to act on your behalf or break through with the answer.

FROM CURSES TO BLESSINGS

This was adapted from a teaching on YouTube by Derek Prince, "How to Pass from Curse to Blessing". Over time, I have reworked some of this. After praying the prayer (printed out here) out loud, within a week, my business almost doubled. I shared this with our home group. One person said that after she prayed it, for the first time in years, she slept through the night. Another person said she has had stomach problems for years, and the day after she prayed this prayer was a great day for her! She hasn't had any stomach problems since. We will pray the prayer later, but first let's investigate curses.

SIGNS YOU MAYBE UNDER A CURSE
(or strongly influenced by a demonic entity)

How do you know if you're under a curse? Two or more of these things might be happening in your life. There are other signs as well, but let's start with these. Keep in mind that not all problems, mental or physical, are the result of demonic influence. Here are some signs:

1. You have great confusion, are you mentally challenged, and have breakdowns or emotional sadness that doesn't lift. Your self-talk is harsh, even hearing in your head that you are not worthy.

2. You have sicknesses that won't go away. You are having the same sicknesses your parents had, or you have a sickness the doctors can't figure out.

3. You have reproductive problems—barrenness, miscarriage, or problems with menstruation, etc. Your sister or cousins have the same stuff. Are you having male problems? (Infertility, impotence, erectile dysfunction and so forth.)

4. You are accident prone. You repeatedly have accidents that end in injury.

5. Money is always short. No matter how much you make, it never seems to be enough. You can't get ahead.

6. You have family challenges: divorce, problems communicating, children fighting or not speaking each other, children hating parents, or your sex life sucks.

7. You have a family history of suicide or there are unnatural or unusual deaths in your family (Three of my family members have died in three separate accidents the same way).

8. You have an unhealthy thought life. In your self-talk, you think of doing yourself harm or doing harm to others. You may also be doing yourself harm with drugs, cutting, masturbation, or other forms of mutilation.

9. You have relationships that find you being abused or have recurring relationships that end badly. The alcoholic, drug addict, or abuser seems to find you, and you want to rescue them.

10. You have had men or women come on to you with sexual desire that you didn't initiate or want. Or it might be the other way around, you find yourself being lustfully attracted to many people.

11. People less competent than you get promoted. People don't take you seriously in your profession. You can't get favor with the boss or the people around you.

FOUR PRINCIPLES OF BREAKING CURSES:

1. Recognize there is something wrong. Ask Holy Spirit to show you anything that is out of line with Jesus.

2. Repent, asking God to forgive you and set you free from all the entanglements of that sin.

3. Renounce the curse, saying, "I no longer want to have anything to do with_____ be gone."

4. Resist it continually. It will try to come back. You will be tempted to do it again.

Below is a good deliverance prayer to pray. I have prayed it many times over the years. As we go through life, we pick up curses that other people have placed on us. Most of these curses were done unknowingly; nonetheless, they are curses.

An example is when the frustrated teacher looks at the child and says, "You'll never amount to anything." That's a curse.

Another example could be the guy driving in the car behind you. What is he saying about your driving?

Some curses are spoken by mom and dad: "I hope you have a child just like you!"

"But Bill, do these things really affect me?" you might be thinking. Yes, they do. Have you ever badmouthed a coworker behind his or her back? Have coworkers ever talked about you? All these can have curses.

I was working at a motel as a teenager. I was putting soda in the soda machine when one of the guests, an old lady, approached and tried to take a soda. I caught her and grabbed the soda out of her hand, put it in the machine, and locked the thing up. She started speaking to me in a foreign language, waving her finger at me. I said, "Thank you," and moved on. As I was walking away, one of her teenage grandchildren informed me that she had just put a curse on me. They were gypsies. She spoke it, and I accepted when I said, "Thank you."

THE PRAYER OF DELIVERANCE

Lord Jesus Christ, I believe that you are the son of God and the only way to God. You died on the cross for my sins and rose again from the dead on the third day. I renounce all my sins and transgressions and turn to you, Lord Jesus, for mercy and forgiveness, and I believe that I am forgiven. From now on, I want to live for you. I want to hear your voice and do what you tell me to do to receive your blessings. Lord Jesus, release me from any curse over my life, my family's lives, or any of my ancestors. I confess any known sin committed by me or by any of my ancestors or relatives. (Take time to confess any sins you are aware of as they come to mind.)

Lord Jesus, thank you. I believe you have forgiven every sin I've confessed and every sin I or my ancestors have ever committed. Lord Jesus, I want to forgive everyone who has wronged me or my family in any way. I forgive them all now as I would have you, Father God, forgive me. I particularly want to forgive_____.

Lord Jesus, I renounce any contact, by myself or anyone related to me, with Satan or any form of occult power or secret society. Lord, I also commit myself to remove from my house any kind of a occult object that honors Satan and dishonors Jesus, the Anointed One. With your help, Lord Jesus, I will find them and remove them all.

Thank you, Lord Jesus, for dying on the cross for me for it is written, "Christ Jesus redeemed me from the curse of the law by becoming a curse for me". It is written, "Cursed is everyone who hangs on a tree." He redeemed me in order that the blessings given to Abraham might come to me and my family through Christ Jesus, so that by faith, we might receive the promise of the Holy Spirit (taken from Galatians 3:13).

I now receive all the blessings available to me and my family. Because of what Jesus did on the cross, I break the power, break the hold, and release myself, my family, and anyone related to me, from any curse, every evil influence, every satanic power, and every dark shadow over me or my family, from any source whatsoever. I release myself and my family in the name of Jesus.

THE PRAYER DEREK PRINCE PRAYED OVER THE PEOPLE

"And now as a representative of the kingdom of God in the name of Jesus I break every curse over the lives of this family and this person, and I release and revoke them from any curses in the name of Jesus, the name that is above all names. I declare these people are released from any curse or any sickness or disease or any viruses whatsoever. I revoke any curses or any parasite and break any curses now in the name of Jesus. Satan, you have no more access to their lives or their families or their businesses. They have been lifted out of the domain of darkness. Every blessing that Father God has for them is coming their way. They have been translated into the kingdom of God's love, joy, and peace. Jesus came that we might have life and have it abundantly. (Taken from Derek Prince. How to Pass from Curses to Blessings.)

Chapter 17
FORGIVENESS

One of the key elements of healing is forgiving those who need to be forgiven: those with whom you are angry or those who have done you wrong. This is a hard concept to grasp.

Forgiveness is for you it breaks the chines the hold you in bondage. Forgiveness does not release them from what they did. It's saying you were a jerk, I know it you, know it and I forgive you. You are not saying what they did was OK. It means that you release them into the hands of God. You no longer hold the offense.

Who needs your forgiveness? If your spouse died, you might need to forgive him or her. How about doctors, hospitals, or the other guy or gal? Forgiveness begins with an act of your will. After you've said it with your lips, out loud, for a while, it will become part of your emotions, and then it will become a part of you. Most of us have said the Lord's Prayer. Remember this part: *"Forgive us our sins as we have forgiven those who have sinned against us."* (Matthew 6 :12, NLT)? Ouch. Forgive my sins as I have forgiven those who have done me wrong, messed with me and mine, or have harmed anyone I know, except for Fred, he really angered me. (I'm joking about the last part of course.)

I was once leading a divorce recovery workshop. I came to the section on forgiveness. There were about 60 people in the group. The minute I mentioned the word "forgiveness," I could see a few people begin to twitch. I knew they were going to have a hard time. After the teaching, we had snacks, which would give the leadership team a chance to engage those who were having a hard time processing the night's talk. I caught up with a woman, I'll call her Jane, and asked her how she felt about forgiving her ex. With gritted teeth and venom that any cobra would be proud of, Jane hissed, "I'll never forgive that $%^&^%$." And out the door she went.

I gave her a call during the week and asked if she could come early to the next meeting. She growled, "I'm not coming to the next meeting." The team prayed. At the next meeting, she came early. Two of the female team members and I had a little chat with her. I said, "Try this. Just say it with your lips even if you don't mean it."

For several weeks, she would see me, and with her teeth clinched together, she would spit out the words. Weeks went by, and Jane began to say it without anger, even though she really did not believe it or want to forgive. After a couple more weeks, the divorce recovery course was over. At one of our singles' meetings, Jane said, with a tear in her eye, "I have forgiven him." And then she said, "I feel like a great weight has been lifted off me. The atmosphere in the house has changed, and my two children are different."

Bitterness, anger, and wrath will keep you in bondage. Forgiving is not for the person needing forgiveness; it's for you, the forgiver. Jesus knew this. That's why forgiveness is one of the cornerstones of salvation. Our God forgave us of our sins. At that point, Father God sees us through Jesus. Not forgiving will keep us knotted up inside. How can you tell if you need to work on forgiving? When you hear the name of the person you need to forgive, if you still get a knot on the inside, or you still get churned up inside, you need to work on forgiving.

Remember *Mark 11:22: "Have faith in God."* Then verse25: *"And when you stand praying, if you hold anything against anyone, forgive them, so that your father in heaven may forgive you your sins."*

This is another one of those verses that hurt. It's clear if you forgive those who have done you wrong, God will forgive you. What's not said is that if you don't forgive them, Father God will not forgive you. That's a little harsh. Try this: if you don't forgive them, there will be something like a chain link fence between you and God. Father God can see you, hear you, and care for you, but your access to God has been limited.

Remember, forgiving is not for the one who did you wrong; it's for you. Your bondage to that situation is broken when you forgive.

Pray this prayer: *"Father God, in Jesus' name I forgive all those who have hurt me. I also forgive anyone else you bring to my mind. Help, Lord."* (That could be the ex, former friends, coworkers, bosses, teachers, brothers, sisters, uncles. That could be church people: Sunday school teachers, pastors, elders.)

In the Appendix is a section titled "Going from Curses to Blessing." I've prayed it many times. When I first found it, I prayed it every day for a couple of weeks. Why? I needed to; I wanted to get it on the inside, in my spirit, and something was happening each time.

Chapter 18
SLEEP

Are you having trouble sleeping? Here's the prayer that I pray:

"Father God, I come before you in the name of Jesus. Thank you for a good night's sleep (Psalm 4:8). Thank you for keeping me in the circle of your love and putting a hedge of protection around me and my family while we sleep (1 John 3:1; Job 11:19). Thank you for your angels encamped around us (Psalm 34:7).

"Speak to me in dreams and visions so that I may know better and have answers to my questions (See Acts 2:17). Thank you for the blood of Jesus over this house, property, vehicles, work, business, and animals." (See Revelation 12:10-11). I bind any satanic power that would hinder or destroy, and I command it to go to Jesus (See Matthew 16:19). Go. Be gone. Thank you for the blood of Jesus over me and my family; I command any evil powers to go. Be gone (See Romans 5:9; Hebrews 9:14).

"Your Word says you grant sleep to those you love (See Psalm 127:2). I know you love me (See Psalm 6:4). Help me, Jesus."

If you have trouble saying "God loves me," try this. Shout as loud as you can, "JESUS LOVES ME.GOD LOVES ME. I AM LOVED." Do it six times.

Chapter 19
FINDING YOUR NEW LIFE

You have recently had the life you created tossed on the proverbial table, and now that "perfect" picture looks like a jigsaw puzzle disassembled. Now you gather up the pieces and start rearranging them, defining a new life out of the old. You must find out who you are without your significant other. Who are you? I believe this needs to start within the first three months. Don't procrastinate. Go for it. You are a mighty man or woman of God. Putting it off only delays your healing. You may be thinking, "I'm not ready." No one is ever ready to start over at any age. If you delay, it will put your life on hold longer than it needs to be.

What are the big pieces to the puzzle that makes up your life? What do you want your life to look like in five years? Find a quiet spot. Ask Holy Spirit what he has planned for you, both in the near future and long term. Take some time and sit down with a pad. Write down the thoughts that float through your mind. Some will be out there. Put down even the wildest thoughts. This is brainstorming, writing down every thought and then going back and picking out the ones that really resonate.

Now do another exercise. Start a new list. Take your pad and ask Holy Spirit, "What are the top 100 things I want to do in the days I have left?" Write down everything that crosses your mind. This is you and your loving, kind, and compassionate Father figuring out what comes next. My wife Kate had a list she called a "Life List." If you have been given only a set amount of time to live, such as three months, it would be called a bucket list, because in three months, you are going to "kick the bucket." If you have years left to live, it's a *life list*.

My list is titled "Goals I want to Accomplish." Below the title is the line, *"Jesus came that I might have life and have it abundantly."* Below that is the line, *"Live life to the fullest."*

Each month, Kate would find one thing to do from her list. Like the day she went riding past the house on the back of a Harley yelling, "Wahoo" with both hands up in the air. I have no idea who the guy was driving the motorcycle. Another time, we were taking a trip up the east coast, and she said we need to get off at a particular exit. It was North Carolina's highest and longest zip line.

Most people can usually come up with 20 or 30 items for their list the first time they sit down to write it. Over time, you will hear of things and add them to the list. Some will be no big deal, such as having lunch at a BBQ joint you heard of in the next county over. Some will involve putting time, effort, and money into them. They will take planning. Why makes this list? It's simple: if you have a list of things you want to accomplish, you will eventually accomplish them. Without a list, you will coast through life not accomplishing much. I once heard a story of a teenager who heard his mother and grandmother complaining about how dull their lives were. He went back to his room, and over the course of the next year, he wrote down 114 things he wanted to accomplish in his lifetime. In his 40s, he looked back and had accomplished over 60% of the list and was giving motivational talks because of all the adventures he had.

Would he have accomplished so much if he had not had that list?

Pray this prayer: *"Father God, creator of heaven and earth, in Jesus' name I come before you asking for you to show me who I am. Show me who you want me to be. Help me to walk in my new life. Show me where I fit into your plan. What do you want me to accomplish in the days I have left."*

I heard of a mature woman who prayed something like this: "I want to serve you and the people around me. Show me what I can do." She didn't get a dramatic response from God, such as a blinding flash of light. She was reading the newspaper one day and started to pray for the people named in it. She found herself in the engagement and wedding section praying for those young people a lot. Was this a calling from God? All too often, we are looking for the big, worldwide thing we can do that would affect millions. But maybe we've been called to pray for the neighbor next door or the people in the cubicles around us.

Now if she had been listening to Graham Cooke on YouTube, she might have written the prayers out and sent it to them along with a prophetic word.

TRANSFORMING YOURSELF

I was an atheist, and one day, Holy Spirit interrupted me, and here we are now. How do you put things into your mind? I do it by repeatedly going over something. In the Bible, it's called meditation, saying it, muttering it, putting the emphasis on different words and doing it over and over again. Weighting verses on 3x5 cards one verse at a time. The Word of God is the only thing that transforms your mind.

Transforming yourself seems like great stuff, but how do you go about doing that? H do you transform your mind when, for years, you have been living in the ways of this world? There is only one way to transform your mind. That is, having a everyday time in the word of God with Holy Spirit. Get a Bible. that sounds like you when you talk. and that you can highlight. and wright in the margins. I like. The English Standard Version., New American Standard 1995., New Living Translation sometimes. For years I used the New International Version in recently they improved it and proceed to screw it up.

My wife likes The English Standard Version with the Passion Translation alongside it, and the Message Bible. She reads a ESV passage then reads that passage in either the Passion or the Message.

> *"For the word of God is alive and active. Sharper than any double-edged sword, it penetrates even to dividing soul and spirit, joints and marrow; it judges the thoughts and attitudes of the heart. Nothing in all creation is hidden from God's sight." Hebrews 4:12-13 (NIV)*

The Word is living and active. The Word can make you stop and think. It is alive. You can be reading through a book of the Bible, and "BAM," it grabs you. That's when you know that verse that was written especially for you. It's like Holy Spirit was looking over your shoulder, knowing what was in your heart, and led you right there, to the verse just for you.

The Word of God is truth. Most of the things in this world are nonsense. My safe place through this whole thing was Psalm 34. I meditated on it for months, morning, noon, and night. At times, I had my phone set to read it to me out loud. It seemed like every time I opened that verse, something applied to me at that time. I read it so many times, it has become part of me. And that is how the Word of God transforms your mind. You will have drama, and your emotions will "swing from the chandelier." Psalm 34 was with me in the darkest of times and in the best of times.

Verses 1-2: Praise will soften my hard soul. Praise opens the gates of heaven.

Verses 4, 7, 17, and 19: The Lord will deliver me from fear and troubles.

Verses 4 and 18: The Lord will heal my broken heart.

 Verses 9 -10: I will lack nothing.

Verses 4, 6, 7, 15, 17, and 18: He will answer me. He will hear me. He is close to me.

"Finally brothers, whatever is true, whatever is noble, whatever is right, whatever is pure, whatever is lovely, whatever is amiable - if anything is excellent or praiseworthy - think about such things."
Philippians 4:8 (NIV)

When Kate went to be with Jesus, I struggled to find anything true, noble, right, pure, or lovely to think about. The only thing I knew was that the Word of God was true, pure, holy, and trustworthy. It holds the answers on how to live life and how to live it to the fullest. I have

read through the Bible once for every year I've been
saved. I can't tell you how many times I have been
hooked by a verse that wouldn't go away. The verse
seemed to be for something happening right then or for
something that was going to happen soon.

Pray this prayer: *"Lord Jesus, help me to become
comfortable being by myself. Come, Holy Spirit. Sit with
me. Help me to live alone, be alone, and call on you
when the loneliness creeps in. Help me to run to your
Word when loneliness grips me. Come, Holy Spirit.
Open up God's Word for me. Transform me into the
person you want me to be."*

Chapter 20
THE DAY TO DAY

You need to manage your time. The work you and your spouse did before still needs to be done by one. Write down all the things that are necessary. These things must be done to keep the family together and make life bearable. Such things like vacuuming, tidying up one room a day and cleaning it. The trash must go out to the curb. On what day does that happen? If you have young children, they will take up a big part of your schedule. This will look overwhelming, but with a little thought, you can handle it. You will find that some things are falling through the cracks. Don't worry, they may not have been necessary. When you feel overwhelmed, sit down for a minute, and say a little prayer. You may feel like you're in this all by yourself, but you're not. Father God is right there with you, waiting to hear from you. The shortest prayer, and an effective prayer, is *"Help, Lord."*

I have a friend who asks Father God to give her supernatural ability to accomplish all the things that need to be accomplished. Sometimes she asks Father God to give her angels to come alongside and help do the things that need to get done.

> *"Do not forget to show hospitality to strangers, for by doing so some people have shown hospitality to angels without knowing it." Hebrews 13:2 (NIV)*

"For he will command his angels concerning you." *Psalm 91:11 (NIV).*

Angels more than one. She says it works.

Chapter 21
WORK

Do you need to work? If you're already working, you should continue. Will you need to downsize your lifestyle? Will you need to move? How do you go about doing that? Get your notepad. Ask Holy Spirit to show you. I think that some people may have the impression that they can do all the notepad work in one sitting. That hasn't been true for me. It's a process that takes time and is still working itself out.

I heard of a lady in a singles' group. She was over 50 years old, and the last time she worked was 30 years ago. Now she was trying to find her way. She was asked to write down all the things she thought she could do. Then she was asked to write a list of all the things she wanted to do or be. Astronaut was on the list. And that's okay. Then she was asked what on the first list was available in her area. She took a job that was okay but not a career. Her second list had "pastry chef" on it. She started working towards that.

My first job was working for my grandfather. The week before I started, he took me aside and gave principles to live by. It has become my life's code.

1. You will show up 10 to 15 minutes early.

2. You will leave 10 to 15 minutes after quitting time.

3. You will do whatever needs doing whether or not it's your job.

4. You will never gossip or talk about, bad mouth, or complain about the job, company, or any of the employees.

5. You will have a positive attitude and hand out positive compliments like candy.

That last one I added a couple years later. I think because of this code, I have always risen to the top.

I have a friend who works for a large accounting firm. They lock the door at 8:00 AM after work begins and then again at 1:00 PM after lunch. They do this because some of the accountants don't arrive for work or return from lunch on time. The company put in a cell phone jammer to keep employees off their cell phones. These are young adults who have an accounting degree but don't have good work ethic.

Let's talk about number three on my list: you will do whatever needs doing even if it's not your job. My first job was working at a company where my grandfather was the president. It was a coal processing company. The coal was processed in a breaker that separated the coal from the slate. One day, I was in the breaker gathering coal samples for the lab to test. When I came around the corner, there was my grandfather with his suit coat off, helping two carpenters replace a beam in the structure of the breaker. He also seemed to know everybody by name. I also noticed that he would walk through the breaker and take time to talk with nearly everyone.

I didn't and still don't like working for someone. I would rather be self-employed, with the ability to set my own hours and get paid what I am worth because I set the prices. Not everyone has this mindset. I remember my grandfather saying, "The one who owns the business makes the money." That's the way it should be because the owner came up with the idea. They put their time and money into it. The workers never see the times when the owner didn't take any money home because the owner had to make the payroll for everyone else. Is it all fun? Yes, most of the time. And then there are those times when you're trying to figure out "where am I going to get those next five customers to compensate the new person I just hired?"

Pray this prayer: *"Father God, help me see the place you have prepared for me to work or make a living. Show me the work ethic that I should have in you. Holy Spirit, your word says. In* Philippians 419. And my God will meet all my needs according to. His riches and glory in Christ Jesus. *I thank you, Father, for every need being met in advance. Help me to see areas that I fall short. In Jesus' name I ask."*

Chapter 22
THE BIG HAIRY A&% GOAL

What is your BHAG? I heard this story from someone in the military. They would have their objective/goal, and if they accomplished it, they can't take the rest of the day off. The BHAG is your Big Hairy A&% Goal. You will probably never get to your BHAG, but if you do, you need to know what to do next. Think big. Dream big.

Have you ever heard of a vision board? Take a poster board or foam board and tape pictures of the thing or places you want to have or be a year from now. Have one for one year, three years, and five years from now. Then have an impossible board. Your BHAG: think big. Put these where you will see them every day. Don't forget vacations, new cars, fun stuff. A vision board for your kids

I have made a life observation. In the years we took time to write out our goals, we accomplished a lot more than the years we were lazy and let the year slip away. Suppose your goal is 100%. That is what you are aiming for. If you set the goal, by the end of the year, you may only accomplish 80%, but without clarifying the goal, you would only hit 20%. You may not hit 100% every time, but you do more than the slacker. The slacker is person who has no direction, no goals, and doesn't know where they want to be five years from now.

Father God has a plan for your life. He can't get you where he needs and wants you until you take the first step. It's hard to move someone who hasn't taken the first step on their journey. Where you want to go at first may be different than where Holy Spirit wants you. That's okay because he will direct your steps if you start moving. Often over the years, Holy Spirit "dangled a carrot," the place I wanted to go, in front of me to get me moving, but in the end, I was someplace different then I thought I was going. Where I ended, for me, was always better than my plan.

Chapter 23
GETTING MY NEEDS
MET BY FAITH?

For years I have been studying faith, how it works, and how to live a life of faith. During this time, I have asked many people, "How does faith work? How do you pray in a new pair of sneakers?" I've concluded not very many people in the church actually know how faith works. The answer I would get most often was from the following passage:

> *"Now faith is confidence in what we hope for and assurance about what we do not see."* Hebrews 11:1 (NIV)

> *"Now faith is the assurance of things hoped for, the conviction of things not seen."*

This is a definition of faith. It's a good definition, but it doesn't answer the question, "How do you 'faith' something in?"

Everyone has a measure of faith. You can say, without hesitation, that you have prayed the prayer of salvation, and you believe that when you die, you will go to heaven. You believe there is a God. You believe that Father God sent his son, Jesus, to earth to die on the cross as a sacrifice, standing in for your sins. All the sins you have ever committed or ever will commit have been forgiven because of Jesus standing in for you. You believe on the third day, he rose from the dead, and he now sits at the right hand of Father God in heaven. This is the beginning level of faith. Don't get me wrong; it's a pretty big first step. There's a whole lot of faith involved in this.

The next step would be believing God to answer one of your prayers. Most of us, when we have a need, reach in our wallet, and pull out a credit card. We end up in debt, and we need help from God to pay off the debt. The more excellent way would be to ask God to provide the need rather than taking matters into our own hands and doing it in our own strength. For instance, every school year, 90% of all children need new sneakers. It's actually a need. The kid's old sneakers are too small, and though they are still being worn, are shabby looking. The question is do you ask God for little things, believing that he can provide all your needs according to his riches and glory in Christ Jesus? (Philippians 4:19) This is where faith gets a little shaky because there's a deadline. School is about to start. Perhaps it's two days away. Now what?

> *"Therefore I tell you, whatever you ask for in prayer, believe that you have received it, and it will be yours." Mark 11:24 (NIV)*

Your situation may be different. Perhaps you put a little money aside during the summer to buy the sneakers. Now your prayer would be, "Lead me to the right place with the right brand that will last." If the money isn't available, your prayer is a little different. You need to pray a prayer of petition. How? I go about it by looking for verses that I can trust until the prayer comes to pass.

> *"And my God will supply all your needs according to his riches of His glory in Christ Jesus." Philippians 4:14 -19*

Verses 14-19 deal with the matter of giving and receiving. Giving is a big part of receiving. We don't give to get. We give because we love Jesus, and he told us to give. The tithe, which is 10 percent, is the more excellent way, but if your situation is such that it is impossible, then I would suggest you start giving a percentage of your income. The reason for giving a percentage is that you can work up to that 10 percent; therefore, if you start with a percentage you are comfortable with, such as 3 percent. This way you can comfortably build your faith, over time, to believe God will meet all your needs even when you're living off 90 percent of what you make. Three percent is where you start the next month, then jump up to four percent, and continuing to work your way up to 10 percent. In our case, it was 12 percent (or whatever amount you feel called to give).

Can you, or have you, ever prayed for something, believing that it was going to happen, and it did? Wahoo! It is so awesome when Father God provides a need. I have an inclination Father God is always working on our behalf, and many of our needs are being met that we don't even know about. It gets a little tougher to believe when you're in the middle of something difficult, and you need an answer to prayer quickly. An example is right now, if going through one of the worst things that could happen to anyone, the death of a spouse, or the death of a marriage, child, or loved one. Are you asking God to heal your missing half? Are you asking God to heal your broken heart, your wounded spirit, and your soul? Remember, your soul is your mind, will, and emotions.

> *"Now faith is the assurance of things hoped for, the conviction of things not seen." Hebrews 11:1*

Faith is when you can't see something yet, but you know it's coming. It's here already; you just can't see it. Imagine your business partner calls and says that big sale you were looking for has come through. The check is in his hand. You can't see it, but you know it's there because someone you trust just told you it was. How is your faith for believing what God said in his Word?

> *"And without faith it is impossible to please God because anyone who comes to him must believe that he exists and that he rewards those who earnestly seek him." Hebrews 11:6 (NIV)*

> *"Consequently, faith comes from hearing the message, and the message is heard through the word of Christ." Romans 10:17 (NIV)*

For me, the message is all the stories about Jesus doing miracles and the stories that go along with them. It's the book of Acts and hearing all the stories of Paul, Peter, and Barnabas. It's hearing the testimony of Bob, sitting two rows away in church, who had a back problem that caused him to limp, is now healed. You may come from a denomination where the book of Acts is treated like a history book. My background is the book of Acts is a textbook on how to live life. What do you do when you're thrown in prison unjustly? According to Acts 16:16-40, you sing praises to God.

> *"So also faith by itself, if it does not have works, is dead.18 But someone will say, 'You have faith and I have works.' Show me your faith apart from your works, and I will show you my faith by my works. James 2:17-18*
> My version: *"Faith without corresponding action is dead."*

I have learned to be quick with prayer. I try to be attentive to people's needs. For example, someone may say to me, "The other day, I was out walking and twisted my ankle." I don't ask believers, church folks, if they want prayer; I reach out a hand and start praying. If I'm speaking to nonbelievers, I ask if I can pray for them. I have never had a nonbeliever say no. Several people have said, "I don't believe in God," and I have replied, "I do, and I believe he heals; let's give it a try."

2 Corinthians 5:7 tells us that we walk by faith, not by sight.

Oh, how I pray to be more in step with Holy Spirit, exercising faith quicker than trying to get the job done in the flesh.

Pray this prayer: *"Help, Lord Jesus. Help me to keep in step with what you're doing. Let me not be caught up by what I see. Show me, Father God, the places I should exercise faith. Help me to be quick to pray for others when they express a need in Jesus' name."*

> *"And Jesus answered them, 'Have faith in God. Truly, I say to you, whoever says to this mountain, be taken up and thrown into the sea, and does not doubt in his heart, but believes that what he says will come to pass, it will be done for him. Therefore I tell you, whatever you ask for in prayer, believe that you have received it and it will be yours.'" Mark 11:22-24*
> *"The one who calls you is faithful and he surely will do it." 1Thessalonians 5:24*

Kate and I built the house I live in. Before the rug was laid, we painted scripture verses on the floor. First

Thessalonians 5:24 is painted in front of the sink in the bathroom. I stand on it every day. Psalm 91 runs the length of the dining and into the living room area.

Are you actively seeking the Kingdom of God and his right standing.

> *"But seek first his Kingdom and his righteousness, and all these things will be added to you. 34. So do not worry about tomorrow; for tomorrow will care for itself. Each day has enough trouble of its own."*
> *Matthew 6:33-34 (NIV)*

This is one of those great passages that states, "if you do this, then Father God will do that." The next verses can be very worrisome. Don't let it be. Keep in mind that worry is meditating on what could go wrong, not what God said will go right. God is the God of possibilities. In heaven, there is no failure; there are only possibilities.

> *"Ask and it will be given you, seek and you will find; knock and the door will be open to you. For everyone who asks receives; and the one who seeks finds; and the one who knocks, the door will be opened." Matthew 7:7*

The Amplified Bible says, *"...keep on asking ...keep on seeking ...keep on knocking."*

The idea here is that if you ask and you seek, you are going to find it. Don't give up; keep knocking on heaven's gate. The Lord God Almighty is for you. He is on your side. He will do it. I am 90 percent sure that the minute we pray, Father God begins to answer that prayer. The problem is there is another force at work in the world, trying to stop the prayer. That force tries to give us feelings of abandonment so that we quit praying and give up.

> *"Then Jesus told his disciples a parable to the effect that they should always pray and not lose heart. [not give up] Nevertheless, when the Son of Man comes, will he find faith on earth?"*
> *Luke 18:1, 8b (NIV)*

I have heard of a group of people called "The Watchman." They have no organization, no president, and no meetings. It's individuals asking their friends if they would diligently pray for their nation, and for Jerusalem and Israel. Their motto is taken from Luke 18:1: "Never give up. Always keep praying." No one knows how large the organization is, or should I say lack of organization. No one knows the beginnings. They have a symbol, which is the fish sign, with an eye made out of the center. The only members I know of are the people I have asked if they're members and the guy who told me about it. I asked if he knew when it began, and he said he has wounder over the years and thinks it started during the Crusades. He doesn't know for sure. I asked him why no organization. He said he thought about that over the years, and he believes the lack of record keeping is because it was created in a time when you could die for asking God to do something—especially if your nation was under the rule of the dictator. Over the years, I've tried to pray every day for the United States and Israel. Sometimes, I have been more successful than others, but for the most part, the job gets done. Sometimes, the prayers last 45-50 minutes; other times, it's a two-minute prayer. Election years need more prayer. I've tried to do this every day. Before I was asked to be a Watchman, I prayed for the country very sporadically. Since then, I have been more faithful.

"If God is for us, who can be against us."
Romans 8:31

George Mueller, The Apostle of Faith was one of the first books I read as a Christian. It is one of five books that I will not lend out, no matter what. In that book he said, "Faith is the assurance that what God has said in his word is true and he will act according to what he has said in his word. This assurance, this reliance, on God's word this confidence, is faith."

George Mueller had a three-step process. When he first found a need, he would pray about it immediately. Within a couple days, he would go to his prayer book, write down the request, and find scripture verses with promises about getting any answer to that prayer. Then, over the next couple days, he would go back to his prayer book, read the promises out loud, and pray the prayer several times, and then praise. He would praise God for the answer to the prayer, thanking Father God, praising Father God for the answer to the prayer, for the need being met. This praising part might go on for months until the answer to prayer came.

FAITH TO RECEIVE HEALING

Are you actively, passionately seeking God for your healing?

"In the same way, faith by itself, if it is not accompanied by action, is dead" (James 2: 17)

Faith without corresponding action is dead. If we pray believing, then our actions must mirror the prayer.

In this verse, we see that if we have faith, we need to start moving in a direction that corresponds with that faith. Have you ever read the prayers Jesus prayed for healing? I typed them all out; it took about 3/4 of a sheet of paper. More often than not, he gave a command rather than an actual prayer: "Be healed." "Eyes, see." "Demon, go."

Here you are, trying to heal from losing your spouse, child, marriage, or loved one. What should your corresponding action be?

1. My first action was getting out of bed every day and making the bed, muttering, "*Help me, Lord Jesus. Jesus is on my side; I will get through this. If God is for me, who can be against me? The Holy Spirit is in me. I love Jesus, and Jesus loves me.*" In the service, they have different ways of making a bed, and one is called "open air." This is folding the top sheet and blanket at the foot of the bed. For most of my life, if I made the bed, I would practice a form of open air, quickly mashing the sheets and the blanket to the foot of the bed and walking away. It worked for me. (Don't judge; judging is a sin.) Some days, making the bed was the only thing I accomplished.

2. My second corresponding action was to make sure I was doing the basics: praying for the family and praying for the nation and Israel.

3. My third action was reading the Bible. I read at least five chapters a day. I chose five chapters because I had

set that goal earl on in my faith. Five chapters a day will get me through the Bible in about seven months.

4. My fourth action was to have contact with at least one friend. This kept me from getting isolated (and helped with loneliness).

5. I wanted to find a scripture verse that would advance my healing. In the back of this book, you will find a list of scripture verses. Take one a day, write it on a 3 by 5 inch card, and carry it with you wherever you go. This is especially important. Don't skip this step. Keep in mind that the Word of God can transform you into your new reality. Fall in love with God's Word, knowing that in the end, you will turn out much better and your healing will come quicker. Ask Holy Spirit what the verse means. Then dial down, quiet your mind, and see what thoughts come.

6. Next, I found two friends, of the same gender, who would pray for me on a regular basis. When you do this, try getting together once a week, usually at church or a home group. I started with once a week then it went to every now and then. Ask them to lay hands on you pray for your healing.

7. Finally, I found a support group. Find a Spirit-filled group of people who are going through the same thing as you. Make sure the person leading the group is a cheerleader, an encourager, loves Jesus, and talks about Holy Spirit moving in his or her life. Before joining the group, ask the group leader some pointed questions. Is this an encouraging group or a complaining group? Do they love Jesus? Are they led by Holy Spirit? Does the group have a dessert time afterwards with chocolate? All are important questions.

Be bold. Be courageous. You are a mighty man or woman of God. You are a mighty man of God. You can do it. Or you are a mighty woman of God. You can do it. I remember a track coach who, before practice began, he would have "head practice." In head practice, he prompted you to see yourself crossing the finish line at least three steps ahead of the second-place person, or at least a foot further than anyone else. Do you see where I'm going with this? You need to see yourself whole, healthy, and living a fruitful life.

> Jesus said *"The thief comes only to steal and kill and destroy. I came that they may have life and have it ABUNDANTLY." John 10:10*

Chapter 24
MONEY AND THE KINGDOM

I don't know about you, but when I became a widow, half of my income was also gone. Some changes were going to be made, whether I wanted them or not. This is the MOP talk: Moment of Pain talk. This is work. It's real. You will need to take a hard look at what your assets are. Keep in mind, the house is not an asset until it's sold. Before the sale date, you have to keep putting money into it. A car is not an asset; it depreciates and needs to be kept running. An asset, in the broadest term, is anything you have that has value and can be sold, hopefully for a profit. Money in the bank, stocks and bonds, investment property that's paid off, and gold and silver are all assets. Write down all your assets. Open your notepad and start the list.

Then start a new list: write down all your monthly expenses and quarterly expenses, such as car insurance. Be brutal and be thorough. For the next three months, write down every cent you spend. Keeping an eye open for wasteful spending. Then add up your income; hopefully it will be greater than your expenses. In my case, the reality hurt! Now I am looking for a lovely, mature, and nubile female with money who is not too picky. (Just kidding. I'm happily remarried.)

Now that you've got your financial picture together, it's time to pray your way through what is next. It took me about three years to recover from the mess losing a spouse creates. You will come out the other side better because of the decisions you make now.

MAMMON

*"No one can serve two masters; for either he will
hate the one and love the other, or else he will
be loyal to one and despise the other. You
cannot serve both God and mammon."*
Matthew 6: 24 (NKJV)

Let's talk about mammon. Mammon is a demon. It has
to do with the sacrifices of children or buying your
children out of sacrifice. What does the spirit of
mammon look like in the 21st century? It is wanting
something for nothing. It urges you to be greedy. It
gives you the feeling of never having enough even
though you have an abundance. Buying lottery tickets
is usually done under the influence of mammon.
(Having said that, and after putting time into this study,
sometimes I buy one lottery ticket when it's really big. If
I were to buy two tickets it would be a lack of faith.)
Cheating someone else to get ahead is the influence of
mammon. Be aware of the influence of the spirit of
mammon. Mammon wants us to put our trust in money,
wealth, and the things we have acquired. Mammon
want us to be seen; "I'm over here! Look at me! See my
new ring! Let me tell you how much it cost me." This
spirit also reminds us of our lack: "I can never get
ahead! Rich people are greedy! I wish I had a new car.
We should take the money from the rich and divide it
among the poor (communism, socialism)."

Pray this prayer: *"Father God, I come before you in the
name of Jesus. You have all provision. You are my
source and resource. I put my hope and trust in you.
You will see me through this. Show me what I can do to
have multiple streams of income. Show me quickly
when I fall into worry or anxiety. Deliver me and this*

nation from the spirit of mammon. You will never leave me nor forsake me. Come, Holy Spirit, in Jesus' name."

Chapter 25
URGENCY: A TOOL OF THE DEVIL

Urgency—*do something and do it now!* Urgency is having to act immediately because someone is pressuring you or you are pressuring yourself. Urgency is never from God. He's always three steps ahead. Except in those cases where he's not on your time schedule. God is always on time. Those who are putting urgency on you are trying to get you to do something right away because they feel you *have to*. I have found over the years any decision that needs to be made under urgency or pressure will probably be the work of demons. I remember the kids' song "Have Patience" from Agapeland's album, *Fruit of the Spirit*. A snail was singing, "Have patience. Have patience. Don't be in such a hurry..." Urgency is a tool of the devil to get you to move without seeking God. If you do seek God, allow him time to get things lined up for you.

Be at peace. Take a breath. Sleep on it. Wait for tomorrow. I can hear my mother saying most of these things to us boys who were always caught up in the, "I gotta have it now." When you pray for something, think of all the things that must line up for that prayer to be answered. People might have to be in the right place at the right time. Outside sources may have to interact with other sources, and all this takes time. We started praying for our next car almost the day after we bought the newer one. We usually bought low mileage, one or two-year-old, previously owned vehicles. In a lifetime of buying cars, we have only bought one brand new special order from the manufacturer. Ouch. We were young and foolish.

Pray this prayer: *"Lord Jesus, be with those who make the car. Let everything line up and last a long time. For those who own the car before we do, help them maintain it perfectly. Father God, get us in the right place, at the right time, with the right amount of money. Thank you, Jesus."*

I am sure glad that I am not God, caring for all the people praying in the whole world. Father God is working for you. He is on your side. He has chosen you. He calls you his child. You are special.

Let's talk about being rich. What do rich people do or think that middle income and lower income people don't? The rich look at money as a tool, something to create more wealth. They have multiple streams of income. They're not afraid to take chances. They understand when you start a business, you have less than a 50 percent chance of success. The chance of you failing in business are great. It's okay to fail. It is just an event. Don't start one business; start many! Some of them will make you money. When I went to work for someone else, I was there to learn the business. I've never worked for someone else even though someone else paid me to do a job. I was always working for my own knowledge and experience, with the goal going into business for myself. I always gave them 100 percent of my ability, trying to help their business succeed. You need to run your life like a business even if you are working for a company. Over time, I have put three businesses out of their misery. I was once having lunch with a fellow entrepreneur, and he was weighing the pros and cons of going into business with another guy. My friend's hesitation was the other guy had never gone through bankruptcy. He didn't know what it was to fail and come out the other side better for it. Having a business that fails is painful, but it is a learning experience. A business never fails; failure is the business owner going through a learning curve. Businesses do fail for many reasons: the economy tanks, the bookkeeper runs off with the tax money, or the owners divorce. It will show you where your shortcomings are and what you need to learn or do the next time.

God is on your side. I believe His method of operation is free enterprise, living in a free market system with as little government interference as possible. You should be asking Father God, "What can I do? What can I make and sell? What can I buy and sell to come out with an abundance?" I honestly believe God does not want us to have just enough but rather abundance (that's money leftover so you can help other people).

A friend of mine stopped at a garage sale with three or four tables of all kinds of junk. She prayed, "Lord, show me what is here that I can sell to make a profit on." She spotted a camera in a leather case with another lens that was full of water, and the lady had marked on it $55. She knew nothing about cameras, but she did know to ask for a little off. The lady sold it to her for $45. She took it home, took half a dozen pictures with her phone, and put it for sale on eBay. After the first week, it was at $100. The second week, as the sale came to an end, the price started to climb. It was up to $555. She started to apologize to the people who were bidding, thinking it's not worth this much. But the price was still climbing. It was one of those sales that the last bid came in on the last second for over $800. She emailed the buyer and told him he had made a big mistake. She apologized for the water in the lens and explained that the leather case and camera looked like

110

it went through a war. The buyer paid the money, and
she sent it off. Four days went by; the buyer sent her an
email after receiving it. The camera, the bag, and the
lens were from the German army. German officers
were given cameras in a leather case with an extra lens
to document the war. Having a case, the camera, and
the lens all together was a big deal. He apologized for
stealing it from her. She was excited to learn she hadn't
ripped the guy off, and she made a huge profit.

Most self-made millionaires do not live in the big house.
They live in a house big enough to take care of their
needs. They drive a vehicle that is four or five years
old. Seldom do they ever buy a new car. They might
buy a leftover, but usually the vehicle is two or three
years old with low mileage, and they drive it until it
starts costing them money to keep it running. The most
popular vehicle among self-made millionaires is the
Ford F-150 pickup. (The Millionaire Next Door, By
Thomas J Stanley.) The working class and the poor
want the government to help them in every way
possible. A self-made millionaire wants the government
to get out of the way. I believe Government's job is to
provide a unified defense of the nation, provide a
common currency and, in the twentieth century, provide
interstate highways.

Americans are confident, competitive, courageous,
faithful, idealistic, innovative, inspirational, charitable,
and optimistic. It's like no other place in the world.
America is the most giving nation on this earth.
(YouTube "What Makes America Different?" Prager
University). The nation itself has given billions of dollars
to other nations to help them get ahead. The USA has
given the biggest chunk of money for the defense of the
NATO countries. We the people of the United States

are the most giving people on earth. In 2021 we gave $484.85 billion. (National Philanthropic Trust. Charitable Giving Statistics) For the most part, we give to the church, and the church helps other people. And we give to charities, such as those that feed the poor. Look at all the local food banks who came through during the coronavirus pandemic. They are all supported by individuals giving food and money. The question is are you generous? There was a season when I meditated on Philippians 4. Check it out.

> *Rejoice in the Lord always; again I will say, rejoice. Let your reasonableness be known to everyone. The Lord is at hand; do not be anxious about anything, but in everything, by prayer and supplication with thanksgiving, let your request be made known to God. And the peace of God, which surpasses all understanding, will guard your hearts and your minds in Christ Jesus. Philippians 4: 4-7*

This is good stuff. Rejoice, give thanks, and praise God for who he is and what he's about to do. Don't get anxious—that's easier said than done. Pray about everything. The secret here is to pray and not complain. Pray for the situation, not the answer: "Lord, here is my problem. I need your help," then again, "I'm still here, Lord. I praise you and give you all the glory. I need your help." During your crisis, expect the peace of God to flow over you, guarding your heart and your mind not to fall into worry, anxiety, and complaining, or trying to figure it out on your own.

Let's get real for a minute. My prayer. "O God! O God! O God! I praise you and worship you for moving on my behalf." Then the next day, "O God! O God! I'm still here waiting. Oh, look, *squirrels!* (They sure have fun taking you down other paths of thought!) Praise you. Bless the Lord, O my soul." The next day, "O God! Help! Where are you? I know there are more worthy people out there than me." Then the next day, "Forgive me, Father God, for my complaining and moaning. Lord Jesus, I know you have got this." And that's how my prayer time continues. Instead of thinking of squirrels, it could be football, my next printing, or some other distraction, like "Why am I always missing the second target in the Steel Challenge?"

> *Finally, brothers, whatever is true, whatever is honorable, whatever is just, whatever is pure, whatever is lovely, whatever is commendable, if there is any excellence if there is anything worthy of praise, think about these things. Philippians 4:8*

> *"And the God of peace will be with you." Philippians 4:9 (NASB95)*

> *"I can do all things through Christ Jesus who gives me strength." Philippians 4:13 (NIV)*

> *"And my God will meet all your needs according to the riches of His glory in Christ Jesus." Philippians 4:19 (NIV)*

> *"Give, and it will be given to you. Good measure, pressed down, shaken together running over, will be put into your lap. For with the measure you use, it will be measured back to you." Luke 6:38*

Over the years, we have made it a practice that whenever we have a financial need, we make a special effort to give a little extra money. This seems to put a little grease on the skids of getting needs met. It is not giving to get. It's a thank-offering in advance for what God is about to do.

Pray this prayer: *"Over here, Lord Jesus. I'm making this special offering because your Word says if I give, it will be given to me, good measure, pressed down, shaken together, pouring out into my lap. My need is _____. Thank you, Jesus, for coming through one more time. Thank you, Holy Spirit, for coming through with supernatural increase. Show me your way in which to increase my income so that I can be a generous giver. Thank you, Jesus."*

I remember hearing a story of a man who was poor. He had two dimes in his pocket, and that was it. While he was getting ready to go to church, he heard this small voice inside say, "Go outside, look around, and see what you can find to give me." Say what? He went out, looked around, found a pebble, looked around some more, and found a better pebble. That Sunday, he put the pebble in the offering plate. He did so again for four Sundays after that. On the fifth Sunday, he had a job. His prayer was how much do you want me to give today?

See the appendix, *The Faith Profession and Favor Profession*.

Chapter 26
DATING

After I became a widow, I was clueless about dating. It had been years since I asked a woman out on a date. Here's my story. You tell me if this is a God story or if I am just kidding myself. Here is "The Meet Cute" (as movie buffs would call it). It's when the boy in the movie meets the girl. It was a warm summer Sunday, and I arrived at church a little late for the eight o'clock prayer meeting. I was trying to get my act together and, inadvertently, left the keys in the ignition with the AC running; the car was off. After church, I came outside, and the car battery was dead. There was not even a chug. I went back in to find somebody with jumper cables. I found a woman who we had known for a year and a half from our prayer group and home group. She had jumper cables. She even knew where her battery was. We tried to start my car, but it wouldn't turn over with her little battery. I thanked her politely, thinking she would go away. She didn't. She stayed until the guy next to me with a big ol' pick-up truck came along and jumped my SUV with no problem. I thanked her again, thinking she would go away, but she didn't. She stood there talking to me. Now what was I to do? The only polite thing to do was to ask her if she wanted to go out for lunch. I did. She did. And off we went. It was an okay lunch.

The next Sunday after church, I walked through the door and our paths intersected. I'm not sure who asked whom, but we went out to lunch again. This happened two more times. One of these times, I noticed that she had curves and bumps in all the right places, and she smelled kind of good. "Oh, my, what a good job Father

God has done on her" I thought. Of course, a good Christian boy is not to have lust-filled thoughts.

I thought I should ask her out for a dinner date. What was I thinking? I was quite happy by myself. We went out for dinner and had a few laughs. I was surprised she laughed at my jokes. As we talked, she slipped into the conversation that this was our fourth date. I was shocked! On the way home, I called Dave who is also my age and hadn't dated for years. He was as clueless as I was. Dave hung up, and five minutes later, his wife Rita called. She asked one question: "Who paid for the lunches?" I said I did. It was the polite thing to do. She informed me that if I paid, it was a date. *Really?*

Over the next couple months, we had several more "dates," and she asked the question, "Are we in a relationship?" BAM! Say What? (My editor wants me to say "I was shocked.") Alright, in my suave, debonair manner, I stumbled about trying to recover and grasp the question. In my head, I thought, "What the H&%$?" I am not prone to cussing, but sometimes I do leak. Then she asked the question, "Are you seeing anyone else?" I stammered around and said "No." She informed me that she wasn't either. Then she said, "I guess we're in a relationship." I sped home, calling Rita to ask her the question, "Am I in a relationship?" She asked a few questions and informed me I was in a relationship. "O God! O God! O God! How in the world did this happen?" I thought. After six months went by, we found that we couldn't be in the room alone by ourselves or things would take a turn: a turn for the worst, or a turn for the "O my?" The wedding date was set.

Here's another story. Bob and Jane planned to get married. The wedding date was six months away. At two o'clock in the morning, Jeff, their pastor, hears a tapping at his bedroom window: "Jeff. Jeff, it's Bob. Are you awake?" Jeff went to the door, and there were Bob and Jane looking a little worse for wear. Hair disheveled and a blouse buttoned wrong... What could they possibly want? Bob says, "Jeff, you gotta marry us right now." Jeff got his oldest kid and his wife up, and they did a wedding. Six months later, they did the public wedding for the moms.

What do I have to tell you about dating? I'm not sure. I know I wasn't looking for a partner.

Here's another story. This one was a nightmare for the family involved. My friend's father, who was a surgeon up north, moved to Florida into an assisted living facility. The father met a woman there, and after two months, they got married! The children were in shock. Three months passed, and father went home to be with Jesus. The estate that the father had intended to leave to his children ending up going to his new wife. The father had a great relationship with his family, and I'm sure he would have wanted his children to have a chunk. Because of poor planning on his part, some other family got wealthy.

Be aware of the scams out there. "There be wolves outside and they will eat you alive." (See Matthew 7:15 about wolves in sheep's clothing.) A friend of mine works for the fraud division of a bank, and she has stories. A woman in her 60s somehow started corresponding with a deep-sea fisherman. They become boyfriend and girlfriend even though they had never been in the same room. She received an email telling her that the online boyfriend had an accident and needed emergency surgery and needed to be airlifted to the hospital. The email requested her to wire $200,000 to an account to ensure he got the care he needed. Of course, it was a scam.

What can I tell you about dating? Be aware! We tend to attract the same type of people as before. If our former spouse was an alcoholic, we tend to find an alcoholic again. How well do you know this new person? For six months or more, anyone can put up a good front. Take time to get to know them. Was your last relationship with a controlling person? Were you abused? Are you spiritual equals? Will he or she still go to church after you're married? Are you financial equals? How will you set up your estate to protect your children? Will you need a prenuptial agreement? Are you in the same political camp? Do you have things in common? Do you have some of the same interests? Have you done a background check?

Chapter 27
GOOD VERSES TO BRING YOU INTO HEALING AND A BETTER LIFE

Someone once asked me why God wasn't healing them. The answer is I DON'T KNOW. What are the healing verses you are meditating on? They weren't. How many healing verses have you put on 3x5 cards? They hadn't. Have you asked God if there is unforgiveness or sin you've committed that has brought on this sickness? They hadn't. Would any of these activities brought healing. I DON'T KNOW. But they can't hurt. When I get sick, I start with asking Father God to show me if I have any unforgiveness or have I wronged anyone. Show me sin in my life. Then I drag out old and beat up 3x5 cards and run through them every hour on the hour. I think and can't prove that I get healed quicker and have less server symptoms. Why? May be the word of God in me.

Does Father God heal today? YES! Does everyone who asks get healed? No. I have seen over the years many people get relief but not completely healed. I have seen people get a complete healing. I have heard of from time to time of open heaves were everyone gets healed.

"Praise the Lord, my soul; all my inmost being, praise His holy name. Praise the Lord, my soul, and forget not all His benefits—who forgives all your sins and heals all your diseases, who redeems your life from the pit and crowns you with love and compassion, who satisfies your desires with good things so that your youth is renewed like the eagle's. The Lord works righteousness

*and justice for all the oppressed. He made known His ways to Moses, His deeds to the people of Israel."
Psalm 103:1-7*

Keep in mind that this was all before Jesus who paid the price on the cross for our sins. We're working off of a better plan then those in the Old Testament times. Thank you, Father God, for Jesus.

Psalm 34

1 I will extol the Lord at all times; His praise will always be on my lips.

2 I will glory in the Lord; let the afflicted hear and rejoice.

3 Glorify the Lord with me; let us exalt His name together.

4 I sought the Lord, and he answered me; he delivered me from all my fears.

5 Those who look to him are radiant; their faces are never covered with shame.

6 This poor man called, and the Lord heard him; he saved him out of all his troubles.

7 The angel of the Lord encamps around those who fear him, and he delivers them.

8 Taste and see that the Lord is good; blessed is the one who takes refuge in him.

9 Fear the Lord, you His holy people, for those who fear him lack nothing.

10 The lions may grow weak and hungry, but those who seek the Lord lack no good thing.

11 Come, my children, listen to me; I will teach you the fear of the Lord. Whoever of you loves life and desires to see many good days,

13 keep your tongue from evil and your lips from telling lies.

14 Turn from evil and do good; seek peace and pursue it.

15 The eyes of the Lord are on the righteous, and His ears are attentive to their cry;

16 but the face of the Lord is against those who do evil, to blot out their name from the earth.

17 The righteous cry out, and the Lord hears them; he delivers them from all their troubles.

18 The Lord is close to the brokenhearted and saves those who are crushed in spirit.

19 The righteous person may have many troubles, but the Lord delivers him from them all; he protects all his bones, not one of them will be broken.

21 Evil will slay the wicked; the foes of the righteous will be condemned.

22 The Lord will rescue His servants; no one who takes refuge in him will be condemned."

Matthew 8:17: "This was to fulfill what was spoken through the prophet Isaiah: 'He took up our infirmities and bore our diseases.'"

Acts 8:17: "Then Peter and John placed their hands on them, and they received the Holy Spirit."

Proverbs 4:20: "My son, pay attention to what I say; turn your ear to my words.

James 1:17: "Every good and perfect gift is from above, coming down from the Father of the heavenly lights, who does not change like shifting shadows."

Mark 9:23: "If you can?' said Jesus. 'Everything is possible for one who believes.'"

Matthew 6:33-34: "But seek first his kingdom and his righteousness, and all these things will be given to you as well. Therefore do not worry about tomorrow, for tomorrow will worry about itself. Each day has enough trouble of its own."

Exodus 23:25-26: "Worship the Lord your God, and His blessing will be on your food and water. I will take away sickness from among you, and none will miscarry or be barren in your land. I will give you a full life span."

James 5:14: "Is anyone among you sick? Let them call the elders of the church to pray over them and anoint them with oil in the name of the Lord."

Proverbs 10:27: "The fear of the Lord adds length to life, but the years of the wicked are cut short."

APPENDIX

HERE IS "THE BLESSING OF ABRAHAM" YOU NEED TO BE AWARE OF

Genesis 12:2-3: "I will make you a great nation. I will bless you and make your name great; and you shall be a blessing. I will bless those who bless you and I will curse him who curses you; And in you all the families of the earth shall be blessed."

Galatians 3:13: "Christ redeemed us from the curse of the law by becoming a curse for us, for it is written: 'Cursed is everyone who hangs on a tree.' He redeemed us in order that the blessing given to Abraham might come to the Gentiles [ME] through Christ Jesus, so that by faith we might receive the promise of the Holy Spirit."

Pray this prayer: *"Lord Jesus I now receive all the blessings available to me and my family. Because of what you did on the cross, I release myself and my family from any curses and every evil influence and every dark shadow over me or my family from any source whatsoever, in the name of Jesus. Amen. Devil, in the name of Jesus, you no longer have any hold over me or my family. I am blessed."*

THE FAITH PROFESSION

I refuse to fear I am not moved by what I see. I am not fearful of my financial future or for my health. Jesus took my sicknesses and diseases away.

God is my source and resource of provision.

He gives me the desires of my heart. He provides the ability to produce wealth all the days of my life. He provides cars to drive, food to eat, clothes to wear, places to live, and everything else I need in abundant supply, which is more than enough. I am not subject to the times. I am a citizen of heaven and I am working off of a heavenly economy. I live in the household of faith, not the dungeon of fear.

My household is thriving, not just surviving. My household is flourishing, not failing. Every bill is paid, every need is met in advance, and every debt is wiped out. I walk by faith, not by fear, in Jesus' name.

Thank you, Father, for every need met in advance, for businesses thriving, for jobs and better jobs, and for deals coming my way. The blessing of Abraham is mine. (Genesis 12:2-3, Galatians 3:13-14)

Money, come to me now. Money, I summon you. I hereby call you to appear. You have feet and are coming my way. I am a money magnet. Money, come to me now, in Jesus' name. I receive money from work, from miracles, and from money-making wealth. You came that I might have life and have it abundantly.

References:

Hebrews 10:35 "So do not throw away your confidence; it will be richly rewarded."

Luke 6:38 "Give, and it will be given to you. A good measure, pressed down, shaken together, and running over, will be poured into your lap. For with the measure you use, it will be measured to you."

Deuteronomy 28:2 "All these blessings will come on you and accompany you if you obey the Lord your God:"

FAVOR PROFESSION

Father, thank you that the favor of the Lord surrounds me like a shield.

The favor of the Lord produces: honor, promotion, and restoration. It brings deals, both buying and selling, coming my way and opens doors.

The favor of the Lord brings love, joy, peace, prosperity, supernatural increase, increased assets, wealth found, and treasure hidden in dark places.

The favor of the Lord gives me the ability to produce wealth all the days of my life.

It gives me recognition, prominence, preferential treatment, petitions granted, policies and rules changed, battles won that I do not have to fight. The Lord gives me great victories.

The Favor of the Lord establishes the works in my hands. It gives me wisdom, revelation, and understanding in all things. It gives me divine health and healing and a long life. It gives me a body like an 18-year-old athlete who's never seen fast food.

> *"Surely, Lord, you bless the righteous; you surround them with your favor as with a shield."*
> *Psalms 5:12*

> *"Blessed in the city and blessed in the country..."*
> *Deuteronomy 28:3*

"Blessed shall you be when you come in, and blessed shall you be when you go out."
Deuteronomy 28:6

"The Lord is my shepherd, I lack nothing. He makes me lie down in green pastures, he leads me beside quiet waters, he refreshes my soul."
Psalm 23:1-3

"My God will meet all your needs according to the riches of His glory in Christ Jesus" [Because I am a giver]. *Philippians 4:19*

"Give, and it will be given to you. A good measure, pressed down, shaken together, and running over, will be poured into your lap. For with the measure you use, it will be measured to you." Luke 6:38

"But remember the Lord your God, for it is he who gives you the ability to produce wealth and so confirms his covenant, which he swore to your ancestors, as it is today."
Deuteronomy 8:18

128

WHO AM I?
I AM WHO THE BIBLE SAYS I AM

I have been chosen to be separated unto Father God. *"For he chose us in him before the creation of the world to be holy and blameless in his sight." Ephesians 1:4 (NIV)*

I have been bought and paid for through the blood of Jesus; all my sins have been forgiven. God's grace has been lavished on me. *"In him we have redemption through his blood, the forgiveness of sins, in accordance with his riches of God's grace that he lavished on us with all wisdom and understanding." Ephesians 1:7-8 (NIV)*

When I prayed the prayer of Salvation, I was included in Christ Jesus. *"And you also were included in Christ when you heard the word of truth the gospel of Salvation." Ephesians 1:13a (NIV)*

I have been marked with the seal, Holy Spirit. Holy Spirit is in me and communicating with my spirit. *"When you believed you were marked in him with a seal, the promised Holy Spirit." Ephesians 1:13b (NIV)*

I am in Christ Jesus, and I have been brought near to Father God through the blood of Jesus. *"But now in Christ Jesus you who once were far away have been brought near through the blood of Christ" Ephesians 2:13 (NIV)*

Father God lives inside of me through Holy Spirit. *"And in him you too are being built together to become a dwelling in which God lives by his spirit." Ephesians 2:2 (NIV)*

Because of my faith in Jesus, I may approach Father God with freedom and confidence. *"In him and through faith in him we may approach God with freedom and confidence."* Ephesians 3:12 (NIV)

I am a son or daughter of God through faith in Christ Jesus because I have been baptized into Christ's love (son of God with a lowercase 's'). *"You are all sons of God through faith in Christ Jesus, for all of you were baptized into Christ have clothed yourself with Christ."* Galatians 3:26 (NIV)

All my needs are met because of the glorious riches that are in Christ Jesus. *"And my God will meet all my needs according to his glorious riches in Christ Jesus."* Philippians 4:19 (NIV)

I am justified, meaning it's just as if I'd never sinned. I have been made just through my faith in Jesus. I have peace through my Lord Jesus the Anointed One. *"Therefore since we have been justified through faith, we have peace with God through our Lord Jesus Christ"* (Romans 5:1). "Since we have now been justified by his blood how much more shall we be saved from God's wrath through Jesus." Romans 5: 9 *(NIV)*

130

GOOD SCRIPTURE VERSES TO PRAY

See Psalm 34 (listed on page 118). It has a bunch of good stuff to pray!

"The Lord is good to all; he has compassion on all he has made." Psalm 145:9 (NIV)

"Give thanks to the Lord, for he is good; his love endures forever." 1 Chronicles 16:34 (NIV)

"For the Lord is good and his love endures forever; his faithfulness continues through all generations." Psalm 100:5 (NIV)

"Every good and perfect gift is from above, coming down from the Father of heavenly lights, who does not change like shifting shadows." James 1:17 (NIV)

"Sovereign Lord, you are God! Your covenant is trustworthy, and you have promised these good things to your servant." 2 Samuel 7:28 (NIV)

"The law of the Lord is perfect, refreshing the soul. The statutes of the Lord are trustworthy making wise the simple." Psalm 19:7 (NIV)

"The Lord is good, a refuge in time of trouble. He cares for those who trust in him." Nahum 1:7 (NIV)

"For the Lord God is a son and a shield; The Lord bestows favor and honor; no good thing does he withhold from those whose walk is blameless." Psalm 84:11 (NIV)

"He gives strength to the weary and increases the power of the weak." Isaiah 40:29 (NIV)

"When you pass through the waters, I will be with you; and when you pass through the rivers, they will not sweep over you. When you walk through the fire, you will not be burned; the flames will not set you ablaze." Isaiah 43:2 (NIV)

"For I know the plans I have for you, declares the Lord, plans to prosper you and not to harm you, plans to give you hope and a future." Jeremiah 29:11 (NIV)

"Have I not commanded you? To be strong and courageous. Do not be afraid; do not be discouraged, for the Lord your God will be with you wherever you go." Joshua 1:9 (NIV)

"Do not be anxious about anything, but in every situation, by prayer and petition, with thanksgiving, present your requests to God. And the peace of God, which transcends all understanding, will guard your hearts and your minds in Christ Jesus." Philippians 4:6-7 (NIV)

"Trust in the Lord with all your heart lean not on your own understanding; all your ways submit to him, and he will make your paths straight." Proverbs 3:5-6 (NIV)

"Which of you, if your son asks for bread, will give him a stone? Or if he asks for a fish, will give him a snake? If you, then, though you are evil, know how to give good gifts to your children, how much more will your Father in heaven give good gifts to those who ask him!" Matthew 7: 9-11 (NIV)

"And God is able to bless you abundantly, so that in all things at all times, having all that you need, you will abound in every good work." 2 Corinthians 9:8 (NIV)

"Come to me, all you who are weary and burdened, and I will give you rest. Take my yoke upon you and learn from me, for I am gentle and humble in heart, and you will find rest for your souls. For my yoke is easy and my burden is light." Matthew 11:28-30 (NIV)

"I am the way and the truth and the life. No one comes to the Father except through me." John 14:6 (NIV)

"I am the light of the world. Whoever follows me will never walk in darkness, but will have the light of life." John 8:12 (NIV)

"The thief comes only to steal and kill and destroy; I have come that they may have life, and have it to the full" [Or and have it abundantly]. John 10:10 (NIV)

"Jesus said to her, 'I am the resurrection and the life. The one who believes in me will live, even though they die.'" John 11: 25 (NIV)

"I am the vine; you are the branches. If you remain in me and I in you, you will bear much fruit; apart from me you can do nothing." John 15:5 (NIV)

"Peace I leave with you; my peace I give you. I do not give to you as the world gives. Do not let your hearts be troubled and do not be afraid." John 14:27 (NIV)

"Do not let your hearts be troubled. You believe in God; believe also in me. My Father's house has many rooms; if that were not so, would I have told you that I

am going there to prepare a place for you? And if I go and prepare a place for you, I will come back and take you to be with me that you also may be where I am." John 14:1-3 (NIV)

"If any of you lacks wisdom, you should ask God, who gives generously to all without finding fault, and it will be given to you." James 1:5 (NIV)

"'Have faith in God,' Jesus answered. 'Truly I tell you, if anyone says to this mountain, 'Go, throw yourself into the sea,' and does not doubt in their heart but believes that what they say will happen, it will be done for them. Therefore I tell you, whatever you ask for in prayer, believe that you have received it, and it will be yours.'" Mark 11:22-24 (NIV)

"And I will do whatever you ask in my name, so that the Father may be glorified in the Son." John 14:13 (NIV)

"Then you will call on me and come and pray to me, and I will listen to you." Jeremiah 29:12 (NIV)

"He will respond to the prayer of the destitute; he will not despise their plea." Psalm 102:17 (NIV)

The Lord is near to all who call on him, to all who call on him in truth." Psalm 145:18 (NIV) (Read the whole chapter!)

"For God so loved the world that he gave his one and only Son, that whoever believes in him shall not perish but have eternal life." John 3:16 (NIV)

For God so loved you that he gave his one and only son, Jesus, that if you believe in him, you will not perish but have eternal life.

For God so loved _____ that Father God gave his one and only son, Jesus, that if _____ believes in him, _____ will not perish but have eternal life.

"If we confess our sins, he is faithful and just and will forgive us our sins and purify us from all unrighteousness." 1 John 1:9 (NIV)

"If my people, who are called by my name, will humble themselves and pray and seek my face and turn from their wicked ways, then I will hear from heaven, and I will forgive their sin and will heal their land." 2 Chronicles 7:14 (NIV)

"So if the Son sets you free, you will be free indeed." John 8:36 (NIV)

THE "ROMAN ROAD" SCRIPTURE VERSES

(Helpful in shearing your faith)

The Roman Road is a group of verses in the book of Romans that are helpful in sharing Jesus with someone and leading them to salvation.

"For all have sinned and fall short of the glory of God." Romans 3:23 (NIV)

"But God demonstrates his own love for us in this, while we were still sinners, Christ died for us." Romans 5:8 (NIV)

"For the wages of sin is death, but the gift of God is eternal life in Christ Jesus our Lord." Romans 6:23 (NIV)

"If you declare with your mouth, 'Jesus is Lord,' and believe in your heart that God raised him from the dead, you will be saved. For it is with your heart that you believe and are justified, and it is with your mouth that you profess your faith and are saved." Romans 10:9-10 (NIV)

"For God so loved the world that he gave his one and only Son, that whoever believes in him shall not perish but have eternal life." John 3:16 (NIV)

Also see the mobile application, "Jesus at The Door." Jesus at the Door is a tool that you can put on your phone so that you share it with people who might need a Savior.

Thanks for reading!

I'd like to take just a moment of your time and ask a favor of you. Would you please leave a review on Amazon? Just click here:

https://www.amzn.com/B0BQ3VFT5F

The review doesn't need to be long. A couple of sentences would be fine.

Reviews are extremely important to the success of a book.

Thank you for your support.

Made in the USA
Middletown, DE
03 March 2023

26144652R00080